For Frank and Amelia

Learning on display

Figure List

Foreword

In this pressured era of content standards and concomitant high-stakes testing, thoughtful educators throughout North America frequently struggle with fundamental questions, such as the following:

- How might we bring the content standards to life for our students?
- How can we engage our students' curiosity and creativity without hurting test scores?
- How might students demonstrate their understanding in authentic ways?
- How can we foster rigor and high standards without standardization?

Learning on Display: Student-Created Museums That Build Understanding offers a refreshing answer to such questions by describing the use of museum projects to connect kids and content. In this readable book, author Linda D'Acquisto distills years of experience as a teacher, museum educator, curriculum leader, and consultant to offer practical guidelines for helping educators initiate and implement a successful museum project for their students. Through the use of multiple examples, D'Acquisto explains the rationale for, and the benefits of, engaging students in researching and displaying their knowledge through the medium of a museum.

To address concerns that such projects "take too much time" or "focus on fluff," the book offers detailed suggestions for targeting important content goals, framing focus questions, determining assessment evidence, scaffolding meaningful learning, and managing the effort. If you value constructivist learning, higher-order thinking, "real-world" connections, personalized education, and teamwork, *Learning on Display* will prove a welcome addition to your professional bookshelf.

—Jay McTighe

Preface

For a teacher, nothing is more satisfying than watching students enthusiastically take on challenging and creative work. While a museum educator at SciTrek: The Science and Technology Museum of Atlanta, I often observed students as they explored exhibits. They were curious about what they experienced and excited to explain what they learned. In our museum programs, students worked in teams and independently, eager to find solutions to open-ended challenges. One such program was a three-week summer session offered in conjunction with a traveling exhibition about the designs and inventions of Leonardo da Vinci. Students between the ages of 8 and 12 studied the exhibition, met an inventor and a patent attorney, and developed their own products. They worked alone and in collaborative groups to invent and test solutions to practical and fanciful problems.

While our students were testing their designs, we teachers were doing the same. Each afternoon we met to review the day's successes and setbacks, to adjust our plans, and to talk about student learning. Our work was as challenging and creative as that of our young inventors, and it was worth the effort—we were amazed by what our students could do when they were invested in their own learning. At the end of the program, students created a small exhibition about invention, which was put on display in the museum lobby.

During the program, we noticed that when students were presented with a genuine problem, they were motivated by the task itself, not by the promise of getting good grades or obtaining other external rewards, as is so often the case in school. We saw that motivation for learning grew when students were engaged in work that had a real purpose, was created for an audience beyond the classroom teacher, and resulted in a tangible product. I was convinced that these principles could inspire student learning in school, with or without a museum venue to feature students' work.

When I left the museum to become a curriculum coordinator for the Fox Point–Bayside School District in Wisconsin, I was eager to see museum education techniques applied to a school setting. The 5th grade teachers at Bayside Middle School embraced the idea of creating a student-designed school museum open to the community. I will never forget the transformation of the 5th grade classrooms during the Revolutionary War Museum project. There were small groups of students everywhere, reading, discussing, writing, designing, building, and communicating their knowledge to one another. Each team was busy with its own work, and no two groups had the same assignment. Teachers guided teams but did not dictate students' work. Rather, students were driven by a sense of personal and shared responsibility for what they were creating. As students were building their museum, something special happened—they not only developed their knowledge of content but also gained a better understanding of their strengths and potential.

Since that first project more than 10 years ago, I have worked with teachers on large and small school museum projects, in urban and suburban settings, and with students of different ages. As diverse as these projects were, each resulted in a dynamic learning environment for students. Students had a voice in what they learned; they pursued their interests and constructed their own knowledge.

Successful school museum projects address accountability demands, explore students' interests, and encourage community involvement; at the same time, they provide students with meaningful, powerful, and memorable learning experiences that demand intellectual *and* creative effort. Although teachers can't make every school activity unforgettable, they can provide their students with significant projects that challenge and inspire. School museums are such projects.

I've been fortunate to have had many wonderful experiences as a consultant, classroom teacher, museum educator, and curriculum director—experiences that have helped me to develop the processes and tools outlined in this book. But it is more than my voice that will advise you on how to create a school museum. You will also benefit from the wisdom of the classroom teachers who have led museum projects for their students, and from the professional expertise of the museum educators and exhibit designers who have made the school museum process more authentic. All of us will offer guidance as you plan a school museum project for your students.

I hope this book will convince you to lead a museum project in your school. Doing so will help your students learn important content, skills, and dispositions—good reasons to proceed. But the project will do more; it will give your students an experience that they will remember long after the last visitor has left their exhibition.

Acknowledgments

I am indebted to numerous educators and museum professionals who (without even knowing one another) have collaborated on this project. I've had the honor of weaving their work together into one "story worth telling"—a story about engaging students in the meaningful and exciting work of creating school museums. Thanks to each of them: the teachers who embraced the idea of school museums and made them a reality in their schools; the administrators who understood what a museum project could do for students and encouraged their creative teachers to proceed; and the museum professionals who generously provided me with insight about their work and thereby made the school museum process more authentic. I'd also like to thank the students who have participated in these projects; their excitement, energy, and pride continue to fuel my enthusiasm for school museum projects.

Special thanks to the original school museum team from Bayside Middle School: Stephen Schneider, Manon Stone, Jane Elizabeth Marko, and Chuck Gilbert. Our first project showed me the enormous potential of school museums and motivated me to further develop the process.

Thanks to the teachers, colleagues, friends, and museum professionals who reviewed early drafts of my work and offered suggestions on how it might be improved. Their wide-ranging perspectives enhanced what became the final version of this book. Thanks to Judy Arter, Jane Belmore, Marti Berg, Mary Pat Clasen, Liz Forrestal, Donna Gerndt, Paul Gussack, Fredrika Harper, Jim Jordan, Kirk Juffer, Pat Morrissey, and Beverly Serrell.

Thanks to the ASCD staff, especially Scott Willis, director of book acquisitions, who was so helpful in guiding me through the publishing process, and Genny Ostertag, project manager and editor, whose attention to detail and skillful editing improved the structure and flow of this book. A special thanks to Anne Meek, who encouraged me to submit a book proposal.

Finally, special thanks to my husband, Jim Stewart, who was with me throughout the writing process. I am deeply grateful for his careful reading of many drafts and for his incisive questions that always pushed me further.

Part 1 The Purpose

1

Creating Student-Designed School Museums

It is opening night at Bayside Middle School. The school is filled with energy as teachers and students put the finishing touches on their Revolutionary War Museum before opening the doors to the public. Student docents are dressed as colonial Americans, eager to guide visitors through the 15 exhibits. They have practiced their tour scripts for a week and guided other middle school students through the museum. Now they are ready to teach their parents and community about the American Revolution.

Community members and parents begin to arrive; their excitement is obvious. They enter the first exhibit, *Colonial Life*, a walk-in cutaway of a colonial home complete with a kitchen table, fireplace, and rope bed. In this immersion exhibit, furnishings and accessories on loan from a local museum are exhibited alongside objects created by students. Near artifacts such as a butter churn, quill pen, spinning wheel, and musket, students have placed detailed text cards that explain differences in the communication, schooling, family roles, and daily lives of colonial and modern Americans. The exhibit addresses the focus question "How did colonial life differ from modern life in America?"

Other displays dot the exhibition. The *Forgotten Faces of the War* exhibit answers the question "What role did women play in the Revolution?" In a dramatic video presentation, 5th grade actors tell the stories of Mercy Otis Warren, Molly Pitcher, Betsy Ross, Abigail Adams, and Deborah Sampson. In the *Can You Believe Everything You Read?* exhibit,

Bayside Middle School 5th graders created a dramatic video presentation about important women of the American Revolution.

the well-known Henry Wadsworth Longfellow poem "Paul Revere's Ride" is displayed alongside contrasting information from books and pamphlets about Revere's famous midnight ride. Other exhibits answer questions such as "In what way was communication crucial to the Revolution?" and "How does one event influence future events?" and "How did the technology of the times affect the outcomes of the war?" At each exhibit, student docents interact with visitors.

The success of this project was largely due to the rigorous and imaginative work of the 5th grade students and the creative teamwork of their teachers, who impressively navigated their first museum project.

A Catalyst for Student Learning

Like all successful school museums, the Bayside Middle School project inspired students' curiosity, redefined the demands of team membership, and encouraged personal responsibility for learning. The curriculum was relevant to students, and they felt a sense of accomplishment and pride when interacting knowledgably with an interested public. Students were motivated to learn as they faced an authentic task that required communication, problem-solving, and teamwork skills. These qualities make school museums much more than interesting projects; they are catalysts for student learning.

Motivating Students

In order for students to gain deep understanding of content, they must become engaged and stay involved in learning. Perhaps the most compelling reason to consider a school museum project is that students like them! The following comments reflect the enthusiasm typical of young curators:

I think it was brilliant. . . . It was really fun because we got to [use] different ideas and come up with what we wanted to do. . . . We put it all together [to] actually see what we knew . . . to put our minds to the test . . . to see if we accomplish[ed] what we need[ed] to learn.
—Bronwyn, 6th grader

It was hard work at the end. I think it was really fun and creative. One of my best days was [writing] the book because it was really hard work, but it was fun showing it off. —Kianna, 2nd grader

Student curators see upcoming work as significant and are excited to create an important product—the school museum—for a real audience.

Students become more involved in their learning when they understand what high-quality work looks like, set goals to improve their performance, learn useful strategies to help reach their goals, and chart progress along the way (Stiggins, 2001). With such opportunities integrated throughout the school museum project, students see that they can do the work and their sense of competence improves. This instructional approach works in many situations, but because the school museum project is a dramatic departure from traditional classroom learning, many students find new hope in the variety of ways they can excel. In fact, in this unique setting many students discover capabilities they didn't realize they had.

Marzano, Pickering, and Pollock (2001) suggest that involving students in long-term projects of their own design enhances student motivation—a factor known to improve achievement. Long-term projects are intrinsically motivating because they "elicit the desire to become more effective as a person or to perform actions for their own sake" (Covington, 1992, p. 157). Certainly, this is true for the school museum project—a long-term, collaborative effort that deeply involves students in their work.

A 1st grader at St. Paul's Elementary School teaches museum visitors about community workers.

Providing an Authentic Task

Students tend to learn more and have more enthusiasm for learning when they are faced with a comprehensive and intellectually demanding task. The task provides an answer to the question that students often ask, "Why are we learning this?" In the school museum project students have a job—to create an interesting exhibition that will educate their community. But in order to create such an exhibition, students must become knowledgeable about the museum topic. They conduct research by reading, talking to people, and studying relevant places, objects, and images. After they analyze and synthesize their findings, they decide how to effectively communicate their knowledge to visitors through visual, oral, and written media.

Like any well-designed project, the school museum provides a complete learning experience. Although the following learning activities are distinct from one another, they are also interrelated. It is the relationship among the activities that makes a school museum project so compelling. Students

• Help define what they will learn.

• Acquire new knowledge by summarizing, analyzing, and synthesizing information from various sources to answer questions.

• Learn skills such as research, writing, and design to acquire and represent their knowledge.

• Collaborate with their peers, teachers, and community as they learn.

• Use their knowledge to create a product—a visual and written representation of what they have learned.

• Communicate what they have learned to an audience other than their classroom teacher.

Each of these activities is demanding. The project—creating a successful school museum—provides an explicit reason for the students to engage in these activities and makes learning meaningful.

An Elmwood Elementary School 6th grader reviews images of the Great Depression for possible inclusion in her team's exhibit.

Teaching Valuable Skills

Planning a museum exhibition is a comprehensive process involving research, writing, design, problem solving, communication, and teamwork. Throughout the museum project, students learn valuable skills.

The Partnership for 21st Century Skills (2004)—a public-private collaboration of leading business, education, and government groups—identifies the skills that will help students meet the demands of the workplace and the global community:

• information and communication skills (information and media literacy; communication skills)

• thinking and problem-solving skills (critical thinking and systems thinking; problem identification, formulation, and solution; creativity and intellectual curiosity)

• interpersonal and self-directional skills (interpersonal and collaborative skills; self-direction; accountability and adaptability; social responsibility)

Teachers are advised to incorporate these skills into the core academic subjects:

> Students need to learn academic content through real-world examples, applications and experiences both inside and outside school. Students are better learners when education is relevant, engaging and meaningful to their lives—they understand subjects better and retain more information. (p. 11)

In the school museum project, students practice these 21st century skills by working effectively in teams to create successful exhibits. The skills, which prepare students for life beyond school, also improve academic performance while in school.

A Catalyst for Teacher Development

Many teachers are interested in developing high-quality projects that motivate students and encourage their understanding of academic content. This book provides a basic framework for school museum planning and instruction, and it offers practical tools and step-by-step advice for developing and implementing the project. As you carry out your project, you will find that school museums not only promote student learning, they also enhance teacher development.

Deepening Teacher Understanding

Seeing students learn in a new context can reshape your view of teaching. For example, the Revolutionary War Museum at Bayside Middle School, described at the beginning of this chapter, provided a rich learning experience for teachers as well as students. Teachers designed the project to reflect the principles of Foxfire, a national organization that promotes active student engagement in meaningful, collaborative, authentic projects centered on students' interests. In developing their project, the Bayside teachers considered Foxfire's core practices:

• The work teachers and learners do together is infused from the beginning with learner choice, design, and revision.

- The academic integrity of the work teachers and learners do together is clear.
- The role of the teacher is that of facilitator and collaborator.
- The work is characterized by active learning.
- Peer teaching, small group work, and teamwork are all consistent features of classroom activities.
- There is an audience beyond the teacher for learner work.
- New activities spiral gracefully out of the old, incorporating lessons learned from past experiences, building on skills and understandings that can now be amplified.
- Reflection is an essential activity that takes place at key points throughout the work.
- Connections between the classroom work, the surrounding communities, and the world beyond the community are clear.
- Imagination and creativity are encouraged in the completion of learning activities.
- The work teachers and learners do together includes rigorous, ongoing assessment and evaluation. (Starnes & Carone, 2002, p. iv)

The development of the project was important, but actually *seeing* these practices in action is what deepened teacher understanding. Ten years later, Bayside teacher Manon Gatford continues to be influenced by her first school museum project:

The museum project taught me to let go of my idea of what students' final projects would look like and, instead, to be open to what they could come up with when given some parameters. I am always amazed. Our team used similar principles to develop new projects, for example a Columbian Exposition of 1893 (focusing on the Gilded Age) and a Great Lakes Symposium (covering ecology, history, folklore, transportation, economy, etc.). Both projects have successfully covered curriculum, helped students learn how to actively present information to varied audiences, and been popular and memorable with the students themselves.

Most of us assume that people change their beliefs before they change their behavior, but sometimes just the opposite is true—implementing a project can lead to new insights on teaching and learning. The reflective *doing* of a school museum project may reshape your beliefs about learning and influence your instructional practice beyond the project.

Engaging in Project-Based Professional Development

There is another way in which school museum projects can be a catalyst for teacher learning—by providing an authentic setting for teachers to experiment with and refine new methods of instruction. Many practices believed to improve student achievement are integrated into the school museum process—research-based instructional strategies, standards-based curriculum design, student-involved assessment, differentiation, and working as collaborative professional learning communities, to name a few. Reading books, participating in workshops, and attending inservice presentations may provide an excellent introduction to these concepts but will not be adequate for teachers who want to apply new skills. Teachers are more likely to incorporate new skills into their practice when they have the chance to engage in collaborative, ongoing learning.

The school museum project offers a dynamic venue for professional development when teams take time to plan and to reflect on emerging student and teacher work. By planning, supervising, and assessing the project, teachers learn new skills in context and students derive direct benefits from their teachers' learning. As teachers work with their team to create a rigorous project, they are engaged in an active form of project-based professional development that is often more powerful than workshops, study teams, or discussion groups alone.

A school museum project can offer you and your colleagues a rich teaching and learning environment. Perhaps the tools and stories in this book will help you examine your beliefs about teaching and learning, further develop your practice, and in the process provide children with meaningful work that leads to deep understanding.

Teachers at Maplewood Richmond Heights Elementary School collaboratively plan their school museum project.

Summary

School museum projects are catalysts for student learning. These motivating classroom projects encourage students to learn new knowledge and use that knowledge creatively. As students monitor their progress and accomplishments, many discover something very important about themselves—they can achieve remarkable results when they persist in their learning. Students explore academic content through an intellectually demanding task, which makes learning more relevant and provides an opportunity to develop valuable collaboration, communication, problem-solving, and creative thinking skills.

School museums are catalysts for teacher development as well. As students become involved in rigorous, active, creative, hands-on work, teachers see the learning effects of the project and thereby deepen their understanding of best instructional practices. In addition, the school museum provides an authentic and collaborative setting for teachers to experiment with and refine these methods of instruction.

2

Collaborating to Develop Museum Projects

Elmwood Elementary School 6th graders Alyssa, Emily, Bronwyn, Tom, Charley, Tyler, and Kyle are installing their *Great Depression* exhibit. They explain that each member of their team studied a different aspect of the Depression and then taught one another what they learned. They are eager to show the objects and images they selected for their display, and they discuss how they adjusted earlier designs to better tell the story of the Great Depression—its causes, the stock market crash, unemployment, and its effect on families. They are still working on their exhibit brochure, finalizing their opening night schedule, and developing strategies for interacting with visitors. The students are proud of their work thus far, and they are very clear about one thing—they couldn't have created this exhibit alone.

School museum projects are collaborative efforts that require interdependent teamwork. Senge, Ross, Smith, Roberts, and Kleiner (1994) define *team* as "any group of people who need each other to accomplish a result" (p. 354). Successful school museums involve collaboration among students, teachers, parents, and the community.

Student Collaboration

School museum projects are *not* science fairs. Many educators consider school science fairs, folk fairs, and art shows comparable to school museums, and therefore useful models for project planning. These events are similar to museum projects in that students' work is on public display. But unlike science fair projects, which highlight the work of individuals, school museum exhibitions (like their professional counterparts) present displays that tell a coherent "story."

The work of a 5th grade student exhibit team from Maple Avenue Elementary School in Sussex, Wisconsin, illustrates this point. The team's display—*Taxation Without Representation: How Did This Increase Conflict?*—included four interrelated components: (1) a vertical time line showing each of the British Acts imposed on the colonists (Sugar Act, Stamp Act, Quartering Act, and so on); (2) a small diorama portraying the Boston Tea Party; (3) student-written newspaper articles describing the Boston Massacre from different perspectives; and (4) a re-creation of a liberty tree, where various loyalists and British citizens were hung in effigy. The team members divided research questions among themselves and used the questions to guide their independent work. For example, the student who researched the British Acts answered questions such as "What was the Sugar Act?" and "How did the Act benefit Britain and hurt the colonists?" Other students answered similar questions for the other Acts. When the research was complete, the students shared information with one another and answered their team's focus question about conflict. They worked independently and collaboratively, divided tasks among themselves, and then carefully integrated their independent work into a cohesive whole.

This level of interdependent student teamwork is challenging, even for students experienced in cooperative learning. Students tend to improve their collaborative skills and dispositions throughout the project. For example, in post-project focus groups, many students from St. Paul's Elementary School in Oconomowoc, Wisconsin, felt that they had improved their ability to cooperate, manage group dynamics, achieve consensus, and solve problems. They also developed a newfound respect for the importance of listening to the opinions of others, trusting the efforts of others, and putting forth their own best effort for the good of the team. One student said that the level of teamwork created a "civil, friendlier environment," as students worked with others whom they wouldn't typically select as teammates. Another student said he became close friends with a few members on his team, something he "wouldn't have thought possible." Several St. Paul's students discovered their own leadership potential. As one child said, "I was a better leader than I ever thought I could be!"

The teachers of these students noticed a fascinating dynamic within the teams. Students who were typically shy seemed more confident in expressing their ideas because in this project there wasn't one "right" answer. Other students, those comfortable with the usual predictability of school, seemed uneasy with the ambiguity of the museum project. (Interestingly, this group included some of the more academically successful children.) They sought adult reassurance and required more direction than teachers would have expected. Teachers said this project allowed them to see their students in an "entirely different light." School museum projects often provide such opportunities for teachers to learn about their students.

Teacher Collaboration

Successful museum projects can and have been carried out by an individual teacher with a single classroom of students. However, there is more instructional flexibility when a grade level, a department, or an interdisciplinary team of teachers works on a project together. A team approach brings diversity of thought, varying levels of expertise, a wider range of student grouping possibilities, and a greater base of support. But it also requires careful coordination of students' work. In school museum projects, teacher collaboration moves beyond the sharing of good ideas; team members function interdependently.

The Bayside Middle School museum provides a good example of interdependent teamwork. The four teachers approached their project as one team helping 100 students to create one exhibition. These teachers collaboratively established focus questions for their Revolutionary War Museum and outlined key ideas to be included in each of the exhibits. They selected a student team for each exhibit, taking into account the interests and strengths of the children. Each teacher supervised several of those teams based on his or her own interests and content knowledge. In other words, for the duration of the project, teachers and students from the entire 5th grade class were flexibly grouped in interest-based exhibit teams that worked collaboratively to create a museum.

Teachers assumed leadership roles based on their personal expertise. Jane Elizabeth Marko, a teacher and certified reading specialist, organized readers theater groups that performed during the opening event. She also developed note-taking templates to guide student research. Stephen Schneider, skilled in technology integration, helped students develop video programs and computer presentations for several exhibits. He also worked with student teams to create "museum-quality" text panels for the entire exhibition. Manon Gatford, an American history enthusiast, reviewed students' work for accuracy. This division of labor capitalized on teachers' strengths and offered students expert assistance in many areas. Students would have received less support had teachers worked in isolation.

Not every museum project requires this level of teacher collaboration. The Bayside teachers were experienced with interdependent teamwork and therefore comfortable regrouping students and assigning teacher roles flexibly. This approach could work for you as well, depending on your team's communication, decision-making, and problem-solving skills. Alternatively, consider having each teacher lead one area of the museum, and wait until your second museum project to plan more creative ways to group students and distribute responsibility. For most teacher teams, collaborative expertise grows significantly during the project—a benefit that outlasts the school museum.

The school museum also provides an opportunity for your team to collaboratively plan, implement, and assess the effect of your project on student learning. This project-based form of professional development is a valuable way to enhance teaching practices.

Parent and Community Collaboration

Collaboration can produce powerful partnerships—especially when parents and the community are invited to share their skills, knowledge, and energy to help create the school museum. Participation in the project offers parents a revealing glimpse into the nature of student "work" in the school. A close look at work in progress provides parents with insight into curriculum priorities, instructional decisions, and the complex process of student learning.

Parent Participation

There are many ways parents can participate in school museum projects. Some parents may chaperone a museum visit. Others may volunteer to supervise a student team, assemble exhibits, create special props for opening night, or find Web sites and other resources for research. Some parents might donate artifacts for a display. Others will welcome the opportunity to offer their knowledge of the museum topic.

It is likely that parents in your community have information, resources, or connections that they would be delighted to share if only they were asked to do so. The Japanese Art and Culture Museum at Atwater Elementary School dramatically illustrates this point. The project was a schoolwide effort that incorporated the work of all 600 elementary school children; it was the school's second museum project. Several families came forward with artifacts and artwork for the exhibition. One family assembled a display case with photos and objects that showed Japanese American family traditions. A wedding kimono retrieved from another family's attic was put on display opening night. A parent skilled in ikebana, the art of Japanese flower arrangement, contributed a display, and a family bonsai collection complemented student artwork.

At the opening of the Fiesta del Arte Museum, an Atwater Elementary School parent participates as a strolling character, Diego Rivera, and a teacher poses as Frida Kahlo.

Parents associated with local businesses made contributions to the project: a professional chef (also a parent) prepared and served Japanese sushi on opening night; a coffee roaster brewed and served tea; employees of a design studio built and donated a wood frame tearoom, which was later raffled off; and a tea wholesaler supplied tea bowls, tea whisks, and powdered tea.

Many Atwater Elementary School parent volunteers came for an "installation day" where they worked together to hang backdrops, affix artwork to the walls, and set up tables for live demonstrations on opening night. The event provided an opportunity to be part of an emerging project and made the time-consuming task of installation easier for school staff. Creating a festive atmosphere—coffee, juice, muffins, and music—can make a Saturday work session a fun social event for the community.

Not all parent participation is this extraordinary, but you won't know the volunteer interests of your parents until you explain your project and invite involvement. The sample parent letter shown in Figure 2.1 on p. 17 can be used for this purpose.

For the Japanese Art and Culture Museum project, art teacher Sonja Juffer modified the parent letter in Figure 2.1 to include a range of volunteer options:

• sharing information about Japan (family photos, mementos, music, artifacts, personal stories)

• organizing opening night activities

• assisting in the art room throughout the year, as needed, with fabric dying, printing, and the like

• building the frame for the small Japanese tearoom

• mentoring small groups of students as they conduct research and write

• providing computer assistance for students as they enter text

• installing the exhibition with other volunteers

• preparing food for opening night

• volunteering on opening night for a shift in the kitchen, art room, or galleries

• educating art docents

The Atwater families and businesses were significant contributors to the school exhibition and provided a wide base of local support for the project. Their involvement spurred enthusiasm not only for the museum but also for the art program and for the school. The effects of parent and community support can be far reaching.

Offering volunteer opportunities is one way to invite collaboration with parents; there are many others. For instance, 4th graders at Randall Elementary School in Waukesha, Wisconsin, created a museum about ethnic diversity in the state. Teacher Randy Kunkel encouraged students to interview parents, other family members, and community citizens to learn more about the history and tradition of various cultural groups. Students gained valuable information through these interviews and, in some cases, acquired artifacts for their exhibits. More important, the interview sessions created an opportunity for adults to tell their stories and for children to learn from them.

Atwater Elementary School students, invited to exhibit at the Milwaukee Public Museum, demonstrate printmaking in the Asian Exhibit Hall.

Figure 2.1
Parent Letter

[date]

Dear Parents,

Our class will be designing and creating a museum exhibition about **[theme of the museum]**. Students will research, write about, and construct exhibits for our museum. We will host an "opening night" on **[date]** and invite the public to view our museum. During this opening, students will perform demonstrations, lead tours, and answer visitors' questions.

We are kicking off the project with a visit to **[name of professional museum]** on **[date and time]** and are looking for chaperones. As a chaperone, you would help a small group of **[number of children]** study professional displays using an observation guide. We will meet with chaperones 30 minutes before our departure time to review the group activity and observation guide. If you are interested in chaperoning, please let me know.

In addition to the field trip, we are looking for parent volunteers to assist with various aspects of the project, which begins on **[start date]** and continues through **[end date]**. Please call or e-mail to let me know if you would like to volunteer in any of the following ways:

- locating materials that could be used in our exhibits
- painting, cutting, assembling—general assisting when "hands-on" work begins
- supervising and guiding a student exhibit team
- creating special props for opening night
- finding Web sites or other resources for research

If you have any questions, feel free to call.

Sincerely,

[teacher name]
[phone number and e-mail address]

Community Participation

Just as parents are a potentially rich resource for museum projects, so are community members who may not have a direct affiliation with the school. If you are considering a school museum about art, members of the art community may be pleased to play a role in your project. These might be individuals and organizations within the local, state, or even national art community. If your school museum is about history, individuals and organizations within that community may be eager to participate, and so on.

As a component of the Fiesta del Arte Museum, the first museum project at Atwater Elementary School, local artists were invited to display their art alongside students' work. One local artist, Jose Chavez, created an impressive Day of the Dead sculpture to honor his deceased grandparents. Through the work of professional artists like Chavez, visitors saw how art and culture influence each other.

Community artist Jose Chavez displays his work at the Fiesta del Arte Museum at Atwater Elementary School.

Professional museums are another potentially valuable community resource. Early in a school museum project, students visit a local museum to study exhibit designs and create criteria for their exhibition (see Chapter 6). For example, classes from St. Paul's Elementary School were given a behind-the-scenes tour at the Oconomowoc and Lake Country Museum. They were fascinated to learn about museum work and, specifically, about the process of exhibit development—knowledge they used when they created their displays. They also developed a new interest in their local history museum. In fact, students said that the program caused them to view *all* professional museums differently, with a deeper appreciation for what goes into creating effective displays.

Many museums provide resources beyond the field trip, and interested museum staff may agree to participate in your school museum project. For instance, professional museums may provide opportunities for students to display their exhibits to a wider audience. The Milwaukee Public Museum made museum space available for Atwater's Japanese Art and Culture Museum. A group of interested students curated a smaller traveling exhibition from their schoolwide museum and staffed this exhibition during a special Asian program day at the Milwaukee Public Museum.

In addition to local museums, professional organizations, and interested individuals, schools within your local district are potential community resources for a museum project. The Fiesta del Arte was an elementary exhibition, but middle school and high school students made significant contributions. Seventh grade students studying Latin American history wrote text for a pre-Columbian display. They sent their work to high school graphic design students, who created 8-foot panels for the text. Teachers in high school graphic arts or technology education programs might welcome the opportunity to provide their students with real "client" work.

Professional Collaboration

School museum projects are characterized by interdependent teamwork—teachers and students collaborating together and with the community to display students' work. Interdependent collaboration is an important part of professional museum work as well. Let's take a look inside one museum's exhibit development process.

At the William F. Eisner Museum of Advertising and Design in Milwaukee, Wisconsin, the curator, researcher, and exhibit designer work collaboratively on each project from initial concept to finished exhibition. *Up in Smoke,* an exhibition that explored the history of advertising in the tobacco industry and in the anti-smoking movement, was the result of one of their collaborative efforts.

Long before the exhibition was designed, constructed, and installed, Chuck Sable, the museum's curator, came up with a general idea—a retrospective display showcasing the changing face of tobacco advertising over time. In this early idea stage, Sable didn't try to "see" the exhibition. Instead, he considered questions the exhibition might answer: "How has tobacco advertising changed over time?" "What cultural and social issues influenced those changing advertising techniques?" and "How have the recent tobacco lawsuits transformed the industry's approach?" He thought first about purpose as he began to define the *point* of the exhibition—the "story worth telling." He purposely chose not to think about display details or even specific content at this stage.

Sable explained his initial ideas to Jamie Kelly, the museum's registrar, and asked him to research the focus questions. Kelly's research took him to the museum's archives, to public and private libraries, and to the Internet as he searched for relevant information and potentially useful artifacts. He found a wealth of information to review with exhibit designer Nils Thorsen. Kelly, Thorsen, and Sable assessed the feasibility of including information and supporting artifacts in the actual display. Some material did not adequately address the exhibition's message, and those items were eliminated. Thorsen, familiar with fabrication, construction, and budget limitations, suggested that certain objects were simply impractical, either too difficult to replicate or too hard to acquire. But many of Kelly's discoveries were included in the exhibition because they were accessible and had the potential to enhance visitors' understanding of the focus questions.

The research phase of exhibit development can present unforeseen opportunities to the design team. Unexpected discoveries—objects, information, and even human resources—may surface and shed new light on the exhibition theme, taking displays in a different direction. Kelly's research led to such an opportunity. *Up in Smoke* was expanded to include an anti-smoking component when his research led him to Bonnie Sumner, an activist for a local anti-smoking group. Sumner was included in the planning and made her considerable collection of artifacts available to the design team. The exhibition approached content from a new angle—juxtaposing the advertising strategies of the tobacco industry with those of the anti-smoking movement. *Up in Smoke* was a compelling exhibition due to the collaborative efforts of the team.

This example shows the importance of interdependent teamwork in a professional museum. Even though student curators are generalists, not specialists—they research, write, design, construct, and interpret their displays—school museums resemble their professional counterparts in terms of the need for collaboration.

Summary

Although museum exhibitions are composed of multiple displays, their varied components present one cohesive message to the museum visitor. To communicate this message, student curators and teacher coordinators must work interdependently within and among teams. Parents and community members should be invited to collaborate; they often contribute substantially to school museum projects. Additionally, they learn about the goals of the curriculum and the work and potential of students. Tapping the resources of the community—museums, local organizations, even other schools within the district—can offer valuable support for museum projects.

A school museum can provide opportunities for teachers and students to deepen their level of collaborative work, for parents and community members to participate in the work of the school, and for all museum visitors—parents, students, teachers, and community members—to learn something new about the museum topic and about one another.

3

Clarifying What Students Will Learn

Teachers from the Alton School District are meeting for the first time to plan their Black History Museum project. There is a lot of enthusiasm for this topic, and even before teachers are seated, ideas begin to emerge. Teacher Beverly Young suggests that they brainstorm exhibit ideas independently and then share their ideas with the group. The room falls silent as teachers write their ideas on sticky notes. One teacher is ready to place her notes on the chalkboard; soon after the others follow. When all the ideas are displayed, teachers crowd around the board and begin to categorize the sticky notes. Their enthusiastic conversation resumes.

One teacher points to the cluster of notes about the Underground Railroad and indicates that this should be an exhibit in their museum. Everyone agrees—there were safe houses in Alton, and local historians would be great sources of information on the subject. Another teacher mentions several knowledgeable community members that she knows, and she agrees to contact them before the next meeting. A teacher points to the cluster of notes about Elijah Lovejoy. She feels that his story must be told—the courageous antislavery message of Lovejoy's newspaper cost him his life. The group members agree, especially because one of the elementary schools in their district is named for Lovejoy. Another teacher notices that there aren't many notes about the Little Rock Nine, but he argues that students need to know more about the early struggles of integration. Several teachers nod in approval. These ideas and many more were ultimately included in the Alton exhibition.

School museum projects capture the interest and imagination of many educators because they encourage student *and* teacher creativity. Most early planning meetings are lively, like the Alton meeting. But how do teachers move from good ideas to a project plan? How do they address mandated standards and assess student progress? These are important questions, as teachers are feeling more and more pressure to replace meaningful student learning experiences with narrowly focused efforts at improving federal, state, and local test scores. Such a shift, however, is not necessary.

This chapter outlines a project planning process with one key question at its core: "What will students learn as a result of being involved in this museum project?" This planning process will help you clarify the *content* that students will learn. Chapter 4 presents strategies for assessing student progress for all school museum learning targets—content knowledge as well as research, writing, teamwork, and design. As you plan the museum project, you will learn how to

• Find the best approach for selecting a museum topic.
• Address mandated learning standards in the exhibition.
• Consider the "big idea," story line, and focus questions for the exhibition.
• Develop statements of expected student learning and research questions.

Figure 3.1 on p. 24 provides a visual overview of the school museum planning process explained in this chapter. Some teacher teams prefer to organize the project before introducing it to students, and others involve students in the planning. Either way, the planning process will help your team get organized for the school museum project.

The teacher rubric in Figure 3.2 on pp. 26–27 describes three levels of quality for project planning. This rubric may help your team reflect on your project plan and, if necessary, set goals to improve its quality.

What Is Our Museum About?

Every museum exhibition is about *something*—a topic, theme, issue, or concept. No matter what you select as your museum topic, it should be interesting to students, support your curriculum, and be multifaceted

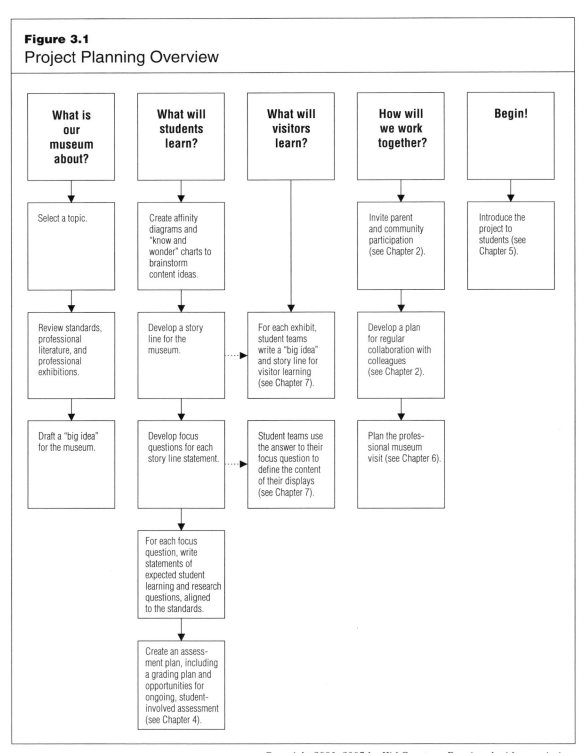

Figure 3.1
Project Planning Overview

enough to warrant deep study. The best school museum topics are typically of interest to adults and students alike.

Selecting a Topic

Some schools are clear about their museum content from the beginning of the project. Others want to create a museum but aren't committed to any particular idea. Schools that fall into the second category may find the following approaches useful in generating ideas for their museum project.

An instructional unit. The simplest way to select a museum topic is to choose an instructional unit within the curriculum and transform it into a school museum project. Using the existing unit outline as a framework, students create museum exhibits that reflect already established instructional objectives, but they approach the material in an innovative and engaging way.

A theme. Some school museums examine a theme from the perspective of different disciplines. For example, a school museum about inventiveness might explore what it means to be inventive in science, literature, art, and mathematics. As students create exhibits that illustrate the qualities of inventiveness in different settings, they make comparisons across subject areas and expand their understanding of the theme.

An issue. Political, social, or human-interest issues provide intriguing content for school museums. Issues such as social justice, racism, environmental stewardship, or media influences are of high interest to students and can be addressed through many subject areas.

A concept. School museums can be organized around an essential concept at the heart of a discipline. Although this approach requires careful integration of content, it focuses class work on significant ideas that promote deep understanding of the discipline in general—an outcome that is at the core of all standards initiatives. For example, a school museum about power, authority, and governance—one of the ten thematic strands in the national social studies curriculum standards—might present different events in world history that illustrate these concepts. Students might examine information from various instructional units and confront questions about the concepts: "What is power? What forms does it take? Who holds it? How is it gained, used, and justified? What is legitimate authority? How are governments created, structured, maintained, and changed?" (National Council for the Social Studies, 1994, p. 26). Museum content could be organized around

Figure 3.2
Project Plan Rubric

Note the performance level that is most descriptive of the curriculum and project plan for your school museum. If necessary, set goals for improving the quality of your project plan.

Trait	Excellent	Progressing	Needs Improvement
Topic	The museum topic is interesting to students and adults. It supports the curriculum and is multifaceted enough to warrant deep study.	The museum topic is interesting to students but is not quite compelling enough to interest adults. The topic supports the curriculum and is multifaceted enough to warrant deep study.	The museum topic holds some interest for students, peripherally relates to the curriculum, and lends itself to superficial study. The topic is too narrow or lacks focus to justify deep study.
Content	The big idea of the school museum generates curiosity among students and adults and clarifies the particular angle that students will take in their study of the museum topic.	There is an unstated big idea for the school museum that eventually may be evident to the students and visitors.	There has been no attempt to identify a big idea for the school museum.
	The story line and focus questions for the school museum provide direction for upcoming research while still being open-ended enough to encourage student exploration. The focus questions add up to a significant and coherent "story worth telling" regarding the museum topic and provide a rough outline of the content that will be studied—content that reflects areas of interest among teachers and students.	The story line and focus questions for the school museum provide direction for upcoming research while still being open-ended enough to encourage student exploration. Although the focus questions don't quite add up to a significant and coherent story line for the museum topic, they do provide a rough outline of the content that will be studied—content that reflects areas of interest among teachers and students.	The story line and focus questions for the school museum are either so open-ended that students don't understand them or so narrow that they limit interest in the subject. Focus questions don't provide direction for upcoming study. They may yield some interesting facts, but the questions don't add up to anything significant about the topic. The content doesn't reflect areas of interest among teachers and students.
	The statements of expected student learning are comprehensive and realistic. They specify subject area content that students will learn in the school museum project—content that is well aligned to the local curriculum and state standards.	There are some statements of expected student learning that specify subject area content that students will learn in the school museum project, but they aren't complete. However, the content that has been defined is well aligned to the local curriculum and state standards.	There hasn't been a thoughtful effort to develop statements of expected student learning. No attempt has been made to align the project to the local curriculum and state standards.
	Research questions are clear and stated in such a way that students can easily pursue their study.	Research questions are clear and stated in such a way that students can easily pursue their study. They are, however, somewhat incomplete because the statements of expected student learning aren't comprehensive.	Students aren't given (or coached to develop) research questions. Rather, they are expected to do this work on their own.

Figure 3.2   (continued)
Project Plan Rubric

Trait	Excellent	Progressing	Needs Improvement
Instructional time line	The instructional time line is planned backward from the scheduled opening event. For every step in the process, there is adequate time for student learning, planning, and reflection.	The instructional time line is planned several weeks in advance, but there isn't an outline for the entire project. There is adequate time for student learning, but for some phases of the project student planning and reflection are given short shrift.	The instructional time line isn't planned in advance. Rather, teachers plan one week or even one lesson at a time as the project unfolds. Critical steps in the process (e.g., learning the full exhibition) are given short shrift.
Collaboration	Planning time is arranged for teachers to engage in ongoing professional development activities, such as examining students' work, discussing research-based instructional strategies, creating student-involved assessment, and differentiating instruction. Teachers engage in peer coaching throughout the museum project to improve these practices.	Planning time is arranged for teachers to develop the school museum project, but they don't intend to use the project as an opportunity for ongoing professional development.	There is no arrangement for ongoing planning time for teachers. Teachers will plan as they move through the project, stealing time whenever they can. Teachers intend to use meeting time for logistical planning, not professional development.
	Planning time is arranged throughout the project specifically for teachers to examine student assessment data and develop improvement plans based on the results.	Planning time is not arranged for teachers to examine student assessment data, but individual teachers agree to examine this data on their own.	There has been no discussion about collaboration to examine student assessment data.
	Individuals and organizations within the community are invited to participate in the development of the school museum. Parents are informed of the upcoming project before it starts, invited to offer their skills and knowledge, and encouraged to volunteer.	Individuals and organizations within the community are invited to attend the opening, but there is no plan to encourage their participation in the development of the school museum. Parents are informed of the project but not at the outset, limiting their level of involvement.	Parents and community members are informed of the project but only as invited guests.
Logistics	Exhibit teams are the appropriate size (fewer than six students), take into account students' interests, and are balanced by gender, ability, and leadership skill.	Exhibit teams are the appropriate size (fewer than six students) and take into account students' interests. The teams aren't as balanced as they could be—for example, some teams lack a student leader.	Exhibit teams are too large (six or more students), do not reflect students' interests, and are not balanced by gender, ability, and leadership skill.
	A museum visit is planned for students to study exhibit design using an observation guide.	A museum visit (or comparable activity) is scheduled, but how students will study exhibit design is not clear.	A museum visit (or comparable activity) has not been planned.
	An opening date is scheduled and publicized before the project begins.	An opening date is scheduled soon after the start of the project—in time to adequately publicize the event.	An opening date isn't scheduled before the start of the project and is selected weeks or days before the end of the project.

these questions to show how power, authority, and governance are defined in different places, in different situations, and at different times in history.

A request. Local museums, community centers, cultural organizations, libraries, and public service organizations may have ideas for student projects that support curriculum goals. Their requests might come in the form of a topic, theme, issue, or concept. Responding to such requests makes the project problem-based and may provide a service learning opportunity for students (see Chapter 5).

An object. Sometimes an object already on display within a school provides the motivation for an exhibition. Colfax Elementary School in Colfax, Wisconsin, had a large freshwater aquarium installed in their front lobby that drew the attention of students and adults. Art teacher Stephanie Ulcej saw this as an opportunity for student learning and suggested that students create a school museum about Amazon River life—the native habitat for most of their fish. Interpretive exhibits about habitat, behavior, and biology were put on display during a public opening that coincided with a family learning event at the school. Like Colfax Elementary School, your school may have an interesting object or artifact that could be further interpreted by an exhibition.

An event. Sometimes school or community events can provide the impetus for a museum project. When this happens, exhibitions support the curriculum and capitalize on community interest in a local event. For example, the History of Our School Museum at St. Paul's Elementary School was created in anticipation of the school's 125th anniversary. The Alton School District's Black History Museum was put on display at the Alton Museum of History and Art during Black History Month.

A combination. These general approaches can provide direction for selecting your museum topic. If you see overlap among the approaches, blend them. Each option should stimulate your thinking and help you select a focus that supports your curriculum and inspires student learning.

Incorporating Academic Content Standards

Museum projects can and should support standards-based curricula. Once the museum topic has been selected, take some time to review related national, state, and local standards. You will eventually align your project to the standards, so it makes sense to have them in mind at the beginning of the planning process. Reviewing the standards can also lead to project ideas.

In addition to reviewing academic content standards, many teachers choose to read professional material or view local or national museum exhibitions related to the topic in order to expand their knowledge, enhance their perspective, and influence the content of their museum project.

Although you will not develop specific exhibit design ideas during the planning process—students develop them later, after research—successful exhibits do incorporate academic content standards. At Maple Avenue Elementary School in Sussex, Wisconsin, teacher Christina Garley and assistant Nancy Gin supervised a student-developed museum about the American Revolution that reflected local standards. The *Colonists Take Sides* exhibit, for example, answered the focus question "Did all colonists have the same view of Britain's role?" and addressed the following four social studies standards:

> 1. Identify and examine various primary and secondary sources of information associated with U.S. history such as artifacts, documents, diaries, biographies, and journals.
> 2. Consider ways in which events in U.S. history may be interpreted differently depending on the perspectives of participants, witnesses, reporters, and historians.
> 3. Use historical evidence to develop and support a position about important political values in early U.S. history.
> 4. Identify and explain various points of view concerning economic issues such as taxation without representation. (From Hamilton School District, 2000, pp. 23–24)

The display included replicas of primary source material—prints, pamphlets, and plays—that represented loyalist or patriot points of view concerning the Revolution (Standard 1). Student-written text described each artifact and explained how it influenced popular opinion (Standards 2, 3, and 4).

The following language arts standards were also addressed as students developed this exhibit:

> 1. Locate information from multiple sources to accomplish specific tasks.
> 2. Use all phases of the writing process: prewriting, drafting, revising, editing, and publishing.
> 3. Write to convey meaning in a variety of forms.
> 4. Orally communicate information, opinions, and ideas effectively.
> 5. Use multiple reference materials and other resources for research topics.
> 6. Show a basic understanding of a primary source.
> 7. Take notes and write researched information in own words.
> 8. Comprehend by summarizing ideas drawn from stories, identifying

cause and effect relationships, interpreting events and ideas, and drawing comparisons between literature and one's own life. (From Hamilton School District, 1997, pp. 17–18, 29)

Because students conducted research, wrote text, and explained exhibit content to visitors, they developed their reading, research, writing, and oral communication skills as required by the standards.

In addition, students used literature as a source of exhibit information, another excellent way to incorporate the language arts into a museum project. In a different section of the *Colonists Take Sides* exhibit, students wrote and performed a short play based on the historical novel *My Brother Sam Is Dead* by James Lincoln Collier and Christopher Collier. In the play, a confused boy overhears an argument between his older brother, a patriot, and his loyalist father. To create this performance exhibit, students wrote a short script dramatizing the family conflict and used it to highlight the differing views of patriots and loyalists during the American Revolution.

Similarly, the students at St. Paul's Elementary School in Oconomowoc, Wisconsin, addressed many state social studies standards as they developed an exhibition on the history of their school. They created four immersion classrooms representing the early 1900s, the 1950s, the present, and the future. To design this exhibit, students interviewed alumni, requested artifacts from parish and school families, and reviewed old yearbooks and other materials from their local historical society. Specific focus questions emerged when teachers examined the state standards. For example, teacher Donna Gerndt suggested the addition of a focus question to address the standard "Compare and contrast changes in contemporary life with life in the past, by looking at social, economic, political, and cultural roles played by individuals and groups" (Wisconsin Department of Public Instruction, 1998, p. 86). In the completed display, students compared the lifestyles of middle-class families of the 1950s and 2000s, and they explored the changing role of women, the changing social norms of the American family, and the typical family economic profile.

Maple Avenue Elementary School students perform a short play they wrote based on a novel about the American Revolution.

After you have reviewed academic content standards, professional material, and professional museum exhibitions, you are ready to further define the content for your exhibition by developing its "big idea."

Student curators from St. Paul's Elementary School included materials from their school's archives in their replica of a 1900s classroom.

Drafting a Big Idea for the Museum

Professional museums often begin their exhibit development process by writing a "big idea." This can be a single sentence—with a subject, an action, and a consequence—that tells what the exhibition is about and explains why it is important. It clarifies the content for the visitor—of all that *could be* explored, this is what *will be* explored in this exhibition. According to exhibit and evaluation consultant Beverly Serrell (1996), a big idea "should not be vague or compound; it is one big idea, not four. It also implies what the exhibit is not about. . . . It is the first thing a team, together, should write for an exhibition" (p. 1). Serrell cites several good examples of big ideas from professional museums:

> *From a planetarium:* "Most of what we know about the Universe comes from messages we read in light."

> *From a zoo exhibition about a swamp:* "A healthy swamp—an example of a threatened ecosystem—provides many surprising benefits to humans."

> . . . *From an art museum:* "What the artists portrayed about the West in these paintings is largely fiction, which had an impact on perpetuating myths about the West in other media." (p. 3)

Here are some big ideas from school museum projects:

• The decisions of businesses, government, families, and individuals can hurt or help the environment both nearby and far away.

• Imaginative people have enriched our lives by pursuing and realizing their dreams in the arts, sciences, politics, and social services.

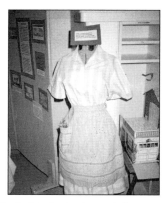

Students at St. Paul's Elementary School addressed state social studies standards in the development of a display on the history of American families.

  • Immigrants built a new life in an unfamiliar land, enriching the local culture.

A big idea will clarify what students and visitors alike should remember long after the display is gone. In addition, a big idea will provide focus as you organize academic content for the school museum project.

Although the "subject, action, consequence" formula is very useful, some organizing teams prefer to develop a title for the exhibition that implies its big idea. Several professional exhibitions provide good models of this approach:

  • *The Science of Sports* (a traveling exhibition about the physics of sports)
  • *Nature's Fury* (a traveling exhibition about natural disasters)
  • *A Tribute to Survival* (a permanent exhibition at the Milwaukee Public Museum about American Indians in North America)
  • *Five Friends from Japan* (a traveling exhibition about the lives of five Japanese children)

The big idea of your school museum should generate curiosity among students and clarify the particular angle that they will take in their study of the museum topic. Typically, when big ideas are well developed, they generate curiosity among adults as well.

What Will Students Learn?

"What will students learn as a result of being involved in this museum project?" If your team thoroughly answers this question at the outset, exhibit ideas that come later will support learning standards and address essential understandings at the heart of your topic. The planning process outlined in Figure 3.1 on p. 24 will help teams define the content students will study as they create their school museum. This process includes several planning steps related to student learning:

• Brainstorm many ideas about what students will learn, using affinity diagrams and "know and wonder" charts.
   • Write a story line for the exhibition.
   • Develop a focus question for each story line statement.
   • Develop statements of expected student learning for each focus question, translate them into research questions, and align them to content standards.

Brainstorming Ideas for Museum Content

Affinity diagramming is a simple brainstorming process that will help to answer the "What will students learn?" question. You may want to use affinity diagramming with teachers and parents to generate and organize their ideas about the content of the school museum. In an easy and efficient way, many are invited to participate in the initial planning efforts.

The affinity diagramming process produces a wide range of ideas that participants eventually narrow down. At the outset, participants form small groups and consider the springboard question "What will students learn as a result of being involved in this museum project?" They spend a few minutes individually responding to the question, writing each of their answers on a separate sticky note so that the notes can later be rearranged. When participants have exhausted their ideas, they affix their sticky notes on the wall for everyone in the small group to read. When all sticky notes are on the wall, teams group them into categories of likeness and name each group with a category heading.

Teachers at Maplewood Richmond Heights Elementary School create an affinity diagram to brainstorm content ideas for their school museum.

Figure 3.3 on p. 34 shows an affinity diagram created by a group of teachers participating in a program sponsored by the Milwaukee Jewish Council for Community Relations. The program included a visit to the United States Holocaust Memorial Museum in Washington, DC, followed by a seminar to guide teachers in the development of classroom

Figure 3.3
Affinity Diagram for Holocaust Museum

The italicized items are the category headings. The bulleted items are individual ideas that were listed on sticky notes.

Springboard Question: What will students learn about the Holocaust as a result of being involved in this museum project?

1. *What was the Holocaust?*
   - Holocaust is a fact; it really happened.
   - How and why did the Holocaust occur?
   - What were the ghettos?
   - How did Jews resist?
   - What role did other countries play in sheltering Jews?

2. *People in the Holocaust*
   - Which groups were targeted for discrimination during the era of the Holocaust?
   - How were lives changed by the Holocaust?
   - What were the experiences of the survivors?
   - What were the experiences of Anne Frank and other children of the Holocaust?
   - How do we tell the stories of the millions of innocent victims?

3. *Anti-Semitism*
   - How do we see anti-Semitism and prejudice in relation to today's world?
   - What is the history of anti-Semitism?
   - What is the connection between anti-Semitism and propaganda?

4. *Diversity, tolerance, discrimination, and stereotyping*
   - How can we appreciate diversity of religions?
   - How do we stereotype today?
   - How can we become more tolerant of individual differences?
   - If left unchecked, stereotyping, racism, and discrimination can have disastrous results.
   - How does indifference support discrimination, prejudice, and stereotyping?

5. *WWII and its aftermath*
   - How does history repeat itself?
   - What happened during the postwar trials?
   - What led to the creation of Israel?

6. *Power*
   - Power that is corrupted cannot bring about positive changes.
   - What led to Hitler's power?
   - How did Nazis tailor their ideology to issues of general concern in Germany (such as national pride, employment, security, and anticommunism)?

7. *Art and literature*
   - Literature is not written in a vacuum; it is written in response to social conditions.
   - What art and literature came out of the Holocaust?

activities. Teachers answered the "What will students learn?" question, which helped them clarify the content they considered most important for their school museum.

Students should also participate in project planning so that their ideas can influence the selection of museum content. Students can create a "know and wonder" chart by brainstorming what they already know about the museum topic and what they are curious about. Older students might create affinity diagrams using the springboard questions "What do you know about our museum topic?" and "What do you wonder about our museum topic?" Teachers of younger students can simply ask, "What do you know?" and "What do you wonder?" and record students' responses on a flip chart. The know and wonder activity—similar to the popular K-W-L strategy—allows teachers to assess students' interests and activate their prior knowledge.

After brainstorming, teachers can examine students' ideas for evidence of misconceptions. These misconceptions may influence the development of museum focus questions, statements of expected student learning, and student research questions. Once the know and wonder charts are complete, students may create a visual web of information that represents what they already know about the topic as well as what they wonder.

Do not underestimate what students may add to a project by discussing what they know and wonder. Teachers were surprised when 2nd graders at Maplewood Richmond Heights Elementary School brought up social, environmental, and racial issues when asked what they wondered about communities. To address student interest, teachers added a new exhibit and focus question to their Communities Museum: "How do communities deal with their problems, and how can people work to make the community a better place?"

Colfax Elementary School students group sticky notes from their "know and wonder" activity into categories of likeness.

The input of adults and students obtained from affinity diagrams and know and wonder charts should provide your teaching team with ample information to develop a story line for your exhibition.

Developing a Story Line for the Museum

Most museum professionals refer to their exhibitions as displays that tell a story. Similarly, as you organize content for your project, you will also present a compelling "story" to illustrate your big idea. Presenting exhibitions as stories is an effective strategy—information presented this way will be easier to learn than information presented as isolated facts. Schauble, Leinhardt, and Martin (1997) refer to the power of narrative in their article about informal learning environments:

> Cognitive research shows that, universally, people can mentally organize information effectively if it is recounted to them in a story. Even children learn and remember technical information if it is presented as integral to a compelling plot. Researchers also recognize that people tell themselves stories about their experiences, and these stories knit the meaning and significance of events they encounter. (p. 6)

So, how do exhibits tell stories? Sometimes they do it quite literally—by presenting a narrative with a beginning, middle, and end. *Daniel's Story*, an exhibition created by the United States Holocaust Memorial Museum, is told in the voice of "Daniel," a young Jewish boy whose happy childhood is shattered by the Holocaust. Daniel—a composite narrator developed for the exhibition—faces some of the experiences that German-Jewish people confronted between 1933 and 1945. Visitors to the immersion exhibition witness different chapters of Daniel's life—at home, in the neighborhood, and in a concentration camp. Daniel describes the progression of anti-Semitism from verbal assaults and public humiliation to concentration camps and genocide. This exhibition is a three-dimensional short story with a powerful narrative voice.

The Missouri Historical Society's traveling exhibition *Lewis and Clark: The National Bicentennial Exhibition* tells the story of the explorers' famous expedition. In one of the first exhibits, *Mixed Motives*, the visitor learns of the charge presented to Lewis and Clark from President Thomas Jefferson—collecting plant, mineral, and animal specimens; trading with the American Indians; and moving the American empire westward. The story's main characters, Lewis and Clark, and supporting characters, the men of the U.S. Army Corps of Discovery, faced challenges—and not just the physical challenges of crossing an unknown landscape, but also the cultural challenges. Hundreds of artifacts, works of art, and documents tell several smaller stories that highlight various cross-cultural encounters. The visitor learns about the roles of women and warriors in American Indian societies and how the American Indians related to their environment. Communication, diplomacy, and trade issues are presented through the story of Lewis and Clark's journey. (A companion book by Carolyn Gilman [2003] presents much of the content within the exhibition, including photographs of the artifacts. This is an interesting idea for students—creating a book that documents their museum.)

Not all museum exhibitions are organized around a single story; some tell a series of stories related to one theme. A Wisconsin Veterans Museum exhibition, *Uncovering the Enemy: Military Intelligence in the 20th Century,* tells the story of locals who contributed to the communication and intelligence efforts of the U.S. military. Alongside artifacts are brief text vignettes, which resemble journal entries and relate the personal stories of Wisconsin veterans.

A story about the value of insects is told in the Saint Louis Zoo's Monsanto Insectarium. This "narrative" includes a set of mini-stories that function independently, with their own plots and characters. One mini-story describes the vital role that insects play in decomposing dead animals and plants. Another tells how pollination by insects provides most of our fruits and vegetables. A third discusses how predatory insects control agricultural pests. Each mini-story illustrates how insects provide benefits to humans—the big idea of the exhibition.

Each of these four exhibitions tells a story. You, too, will define the "story worth telling" for your school museum by writing a story line—a set of statements that expand on your big idea and outline what visitors will learn in the exhibition. To write the story line, teachers use what they have learned from their review of professional museum exhibitions, professional literature, related curriculum unit objectives, academic content standards, and brainstorming activities. Consider how the following story line supports the big idea of a school exhibition on immigration:

Big idea: Immigrants built a new life in an unfamiliar land, enriching the local culture.

Story line:

1. People came from faraway lands to Wisconsin.
2. Compared to life in their native lands, life for immigrants in Wisconsin was very different in some ways and the same in other ways.

3. Immigrating to another country is exciting and difficult.
4. Some cultural groups experienced stereotyping or discrimination.
5. Each cultural group is unique and enriches the local culture.

As in this example, your story line statements should outline the important aspects of your museum topic and support your big idea. These statements organize museum content in a meaningful way and assure coherence within the completed exhibition.

Developing Focus Questions

Teachers create story lines to ensure that the content of their upcoming exhibition is coherent, reflects students' interests, incorporates standards, and addresses other important information they have reviewed. Teachers use their completed story line to develop a set of focus questions that student exhibit teams will explore. These focus questions, derived from the story line, provide exhibit teams with direction for study. Consider the Immigration Museum example:

Story line:	People came from faraway lands to Wisconsin.
Focus question:	What brought people from faraway lands to Wisconsin?
Story line:	Compared to life in their native lands, life for immigrants in Wisconsin was very different in some ways and the same in other ways.
Focus question:	How has life changed and stayed the same for cultural groups that immigrated to Wisconsin?
Story line:	Immigrating to another country is exciting and difficult.
Focus question:	What is it like to immigrate to another country?
Story line:	Some cultural groups experienced stereotyping or discrimination.
Focus question:	What forms of stereotyping or discrimination have different cultural groups experienced?
Story line:	Each cultural group is unique and enriches the local culture.
Focus question:	How has each cultural group enriched the local culture where they settled?

The length of your story line and the number of focus questions in your exhibition will depend on the number of students who will be on exhibit teams. Typically, teachers assign a group of four to five students one focus question that has a number of avenues for research. Sometimes—especially with young students—an entire classroom will research one focus question in great depth.

Focus questions are similar to unit questions in the Understanding by Design model (Wiggins & McTighe, 1998, p. 30), which frame particular content and inquiry. Like unit questions, focus questions

• Are specific to subject areas but point to essential questions and big ideas.
   • Have no one "correct" answer.
   • Are designed to generate and maintain student interest.

Focus questions are open-ended by design; a question with a simple, well-understood answer would provide little challenge or motivation for students. There is never one "right" way to approach the questions—students are free to pursue any number of potentially successful outcomes. This means that all students can be successful and succeed in a variety of ways.

After you have developed your story line and focus questions, consider whether they offer enough direction and challenge for students' upcoming research. Are your story line and focus questions open-ended enough to encourage exploration? Do they add up to a significant and coherent "story worth telling" regarding your museum topic? Do they provide a rough outline of the content that students will study? Does this content reflect areas of interest among teachers and students? If you are satisfied with your story line and focus questions, you are ready to move on.

Writing Statements of Expected Student Learning and Research Questions

Statements of expected student learning specify the important ideas and concepts that you would like students to learn as they explore their focus question. These statements are typically not shared with students; teachers use them to develop research questions. Some teachers feel that by first developing statements of expected student learning, they are better able to write research questions that target important areas of student learning.

For example, based on the affinity diagram in Figure 3.3 on p. 34, teachers would write a story line for their Holocaust exhibition and develop corresponding focus questions. One focus question might be "Who were the victims in the era of the Holocaust?" From this question, teachers might develop statements of expected student learning like those listed in Column 1 of Figure 3.4 (see p. 40). These statements clarify what the exhibit team members will learn as they research their focus question. Be sure to review your statements of expected student learning to make sure that they are comprehensive and specific.

The statements of expected student learning can easily be translated into corresponding research questions, as shown in Column 2 of Figure 3.4. Research questions provide another level of detail as exhibit teams explore their focus question. The research questions should provide direction for students' upcoming study, although students will likely add their own questions as they conduct research.

Aligning the Project with the Standards

If you began with a review of the standards before writing your big idea, their influence should be clearly present as your museum project takes shape. As a final check to make sure the project addresses the standards, complete an alignment table for each focus question. Column 3 in Figure 3.4 shows standards related to the statements of expected student learning for the focus question "Who were the victims in the era of the Holocaust?"

Figure 3.4
Standards Alignment for Holocaust Museum

Exhibit Focus Question: Who were the victims in the era of the Holocaust?

Statements of Expected Student Learning	Student Research Questions	Related State Standards
Different groups were persecuted in the era of the Holocaust.	What groups were persecuted in the era of the Holocaust? Why were they selected for persecution?	History standards (Wisconsin Department of Public Instruction, 1998, p. 87): • B.8.1 Interpret the past using a variety of sources, such as biographies, diaries, journals, artifacts, eyewitness interviews, and other primary materials, and evaluate the credibility of sources used.
Children such as Anne Frank interpreted the Holocaust from their unique perspectives.	Who was Anne Frank? What were her experiences during the Holocaust? What were the experiences of other children?	• B.8.4 Explain how and why events may be interpreted differently depending upon the perspectives of participants, witnesses, reporters, and historians. • B.8.7 Identify significant events and people in the major eras of United States and world history.
The oral and written histories of survivors help us understand the effect of the Holocaust on the lives and families of those persecuted.	Where are the oral and written histories of Holocaust survivors kept? According to the oral and written histories you find, what effect did the Holocaust have on the lives and families of those persecuted?	• B.8.10 Analyze examples of conflict, cooperation, and interdependence among groups, societies, or nations. Behavioral sciences standards (Wisconsin Department of Public Instruction, 1998, p. 97): • E.8.7 Identify and explain examples of bias, prejudice, and stereotyping, and how they contribute to conflict in a society.

A set of sample agendas is provided in Appendix A to guide your team through the project planning process. As you engage in these activities, remember that they are the first steps in designing a standards-based project; alignment will continue as you develop assessments and instructional activities. Curriculum design frameworks such as Understanding by Design (Wiggins & McTighe, 1998) present an instructional planning process in which teachers first define what students will learn, then design assessments to provide evidence that students have learned, and finally plan instructional activities that provide opportunities for students to learn. This design strategy works very well when teachers are careful to align standards, assessment, and instructional activities *throughout* the school museum planning process.

Summary

School museums may be about curriculum topics; interdisciplinary themes; political, social, or human-interest issues; concepts central to a discipline; community requests; objects or artifacts; local events; or some combination of the above. Teachers align the museum project with state and local standards, ensuring that it supports defined curricular objectives. As they develop the content for the exhibition, they draft a "big idea"—a statement that explains why a museum topic is significant and clarifies what content will be included.

An important question—"What will students learn as a result of being involved in this museum project?"—is at the heart of project planning for a school museum. Affinity diagrams and "know and wonder" charts allow teachers, students, and parents to respond to this question, providing valuable input for the organizing team. Teachers use this information to define the "story worth telling," the story line that will shape the exhibition and upcoming work. From the story line, teachers develop focus questions, which provide direction for subsequent student research and expected learning.

4

Assessing Student Learning

Fourth grade teachers Maya, Eva, Marcus, and Adrian are meeting in the teacher workroom to plan assessment activities for their museum project. They review the grading plan they developed last week; they selected 10 items that they will use to determine a final grade for the project. Adrian worries that their grading plan may not provide enough evidence of student achievement for each of the project learning targets. Maya suggests a solution—they could use the research, exhibit design, and label copy rubrics to grade their students' work multiple times throughout the project. There is a pause as teachers consider this option. Eva isn't sure that Maya's idea would be fair to students. Teachers expect students' initial work to be less proficient than their completed work. She wonders if teachers should record students' practice attempts in the grade book; doing so might discourage students from using rubrics to improve their work.

After some discussion, the teachers decide to use the rubrics as improvement tools throughout the project and as grading tools only after students submit their final work. This distinction reassures Adrian about their 10-item grading plan. Because they will provide ongoing assessment throughout the project, the teachers feel confident that they will have ample evidence of student progress. They will stick with their grading plan but agree to revisit the issue in three weeks.

These teachers are creating a classroom assessment plan that will do two important things: measure what students know and can do, and provide opportunities for students to monitor their own progress along the way. High-quality plans balance summative assessments, which measure student learning, and student-involved formative assessments, which are designed to improve instruction and student performance. As Wiggins (1998) suggests, educative assessment is a system that "is deliberately designed to teach and improve, not just measure" (p. 21).

This chapter discusses strategies for creating a high-quality assessment plan for your school museum project that involves students in the assessment process and balances summative and formative assessment. This plan should provide you with sufficient evidence that your students have achieved the learning targets outlined in your museum project. It should also include opportunities for students to monitor their work in progress and communicate about their emerging proficiency.

In the school museum project, students are assessed on their exhibit's organization, content, presentation, and effect.

The teacher rubric in Figure 4.1 on p. 44 describes three levels of quality for assessment plans. This rubric may help your team reflect on your assessment plan and, if necessary, set goals to improve its quality.

Defining Learning Targets

"What did students learn as a result of being involved in this museum project?" This is a summative assessment question. You will answer it later in the project, when it is appropriate to determine what students have learned. Before you can answer this question, you must be clear about what you expect students to learn; you must define the project's learning targets.

Perhaps you are saying, "Didn't we just do that in Chapter 3?" Yes, you established exhibit focus questions and student research questions, all aligned to content standards related to your museum topic. Now step back and ask a larger achievement question: "What are *all* the learning targets we expect students to hit in this standards-based museum project?" Certainly, academic content standards related to your topic are a large part of the answer. But you will assess learning targets beyond academic content knowledge—skills related to research,

Figure 4.1

Assessment Plan Rubric

Note the performance level that is most descriptive of the assessment plan for your school museum. If necessary, set goals for improving the quality of your assessment plan.

Trait	Excellent	Progressing	Needs Improvement
Student learning targets	The learning targets are written in language that students understand.	The learning targets are clear to teachers, but there is no plan to present them to students.	The learning targets aren't identified.
	There is a plan to provide students with examples of high-quality work for all learning targets so that they develop a vision of quality for these areas.	There is a plan to provide students with examples of high-quality work for some learning targets, but adequate time isn't allotted to do this for all targets.	Students don't examine examples of high-quality work for the learning targets.
	The content targets—the statements of expected student learning—are comprehensive.	The content targets—the statements of expected student learning—exist for some but not all focus questions.	The content targets—the statements of expected student learning—exist for very few or no focus questions.
Student-involved formative assessment	For all targets, assessment activities are integrated into the instructional plan to help students understand quality work, compare their work to the standard, and improve their performance.	For some targets, assessment activities are integrated into the instructional plan to help students understand quality work, compare their work to the standard, and improve their performance.	Very few assessment activities are integrated into the instructional plan. Students don't fully understand quality work, are unable to compare their work to a standard, and have difficulty knowing how to improve their performance.
	Time is allotted to provide students with frequent descriptive feedback so that they know how to improve their performance for all targets.	Time is allotted to provide students with descriptive feedback so that they know how to improve their performance for some targets.	Little time is allotted to provide students with descriptive feedback. Students don't know how to improve their performance.
	Students use work samples to explain progress toward all learning targets.	Students use work samples to explain progress toward some learning targets.	Students use work samples to explain progress toward very few learning targets.
Grading plan	The grading plan includes summative assessments that show student achievement for all learning targets.	The grading plan includes summative assessments that show student achievement for some learning targets, but there isn't time to collect this evidence for all targets.	The grading plan includes some summative assessments, but they aren't well aligned to the learning targets.
	Student performance on all learning targets is measured by using an appropriate assessment method—selected/constructed response test, extended written response test, performance assessment, or personal communication.	Student performance on most learning targets is measured by using an appropriate assessment method—selected/constructed response test, extended written response test, performance assessment, or personal communication.	There isn't always a good match between the learning targets and an appropriate assessment method—selected/constructed response test, extended written response test, performance assessment, or personal communication.
	There is a student-friendly version of the grading plan that shows how student performance will be measured and grades will be calculated. "Scores" on formative assessments and practice work are not included in the grading plan. Grades are based on summative assessments.	There is a grading plan that shows how student performance will be measured and grades will be calculated, but it is primarily used by teachers, not students. The grading plan includes some formative assessments and some practice work calculated into the final grade.	There isn't a grading plan to show how student performance will be measured. It is possible that everything a student does will be given a score and every score will be included in the grading plan, including formative assessments and practice work.

reasoning, writing, teamwork, and exhibit design. Clarifying these learning targets is a critical step in developing a good assessment plan.

First, you will need to define the *types* of achievement targets you will assess. Consider the four types of learning targets suggested by Stiggins, Arter, Chappuis, and Chappuis (2004, pp. 61–75):

- *Knowledge:* Student knows core facts and concepts.
- *Reasoning:* Student uses knowledge to reason and solve problems. The student may induce, deduce, analyze, compare, classify, evaluate, or synthesize.
- *Performance skills:* Student uses knowledge and reasoning while performing skillfully (reading fluently, working productively, carrying out science investigations, and so on).
- *Products:* Student creates quality products (museum exhibits, science fair displays, term papers, artwork, and the like) that require use of knowledge, reasoning, and performance skills.

Notice how the learning targets grow in sophistication—knowledge at the lower end of the continuum, product at the higher end. This progression makes sense; it is not possible to create a product without using knowledge, reasoning, and performance skills.

Complex tasks, such as creating a school museum, require that students *use* knowledge in a realistic context. Students working on the museum project are responsible for developing a product that demonstrates their knowledge, reasoning, and skill. They are also responsible for demonstrating achievement within each of the other learning targets for the school museum project:

- *Knowledge:* Student is able to answer each of the focus questions in the school museum (student as content expert).
- *Reasoning:* Student uses multiple resources to find relevant information and synthesizes research notes to answer research and focus questions (student as researcher).
- *Performance skills:* Student interacts effectively with museum visitors, explaining exhibit content and actively engaging visitors in learning (student as skilled communicator). Student works effectively on a team (student as team player).
- *Products:* Student writes appropriate label copy that describes exhibit artifacts and answers research and focus questions (student as writer). Student designs appealing, effective, informative displays that answer focus questions and engage visitors (student as exhibit designer).

Clear learning targets provide direction for your students' work. Before introducing the project to your students (see Chapter 5), consider writing the targets in language they will understand. Stiggins and colleagues (2004, pp. 58–59) suggest a process for translating standards (or learning targets) into "I can" statements. The process is simple: (1) Select the learning target that students will have difficulty understanding; (2) identify the words that need clarification and define them; and (3) rewrite the target as an "I can" or "I am learning to" statement. For example, the learning target "use multiple resources to find relevant information and synthesize research notes to answer research and focus questions" might be difficult for younger students to understand. You might rewrite the target as follows: "I can get information from people, places, books, and the Internet and use it to answer my research and focus questions."

Selecting Assessment Methods

After you have defined the type of learning targets you will assess, you will need to choose a method of assessment. The following methods are used by most classroom teachers (Stiggins et al., 2004, pp. 90–93):

• *Selected/constructed response:* Students select the best response from a list. Formats include multiple choice, true/false, matching, short answer, and fill in the blank.

• *Extended written response:* Students construct an extended written answer in response to a question or task.

• *Performance assessment:* Students create a complex performance or product in response to a task that may simulate real-world problems or challenges, that includes higher-order thinking skills, and that has specific scoring guides or rubrics. These assessments measure the effective application of knowledge and skill.

• *Personal communication:* Students interact with the teacher, orally or in writing. Questions may be posed and answered through interviews, conferences, conversations, oral examinations, or by responding to student comments in journals and logs.

Although most teachers will recognize such achievement targets and assessment methods, matching methods to targets requires careful thought. The skillful assessor recognizes that not all methods work well for all targets (Stiggins et al., 2004, p. 100). The matrix in Figure 4.2 on pp. 48–49 illustrates the match between method and target in general and as applied to a school museum project. The matrix may help you decide how you will evaluate students during the museum project, and you can use it to develop a grading plan to share with your students. Figure 4.3 on p. 50 is an example of a grading plan that matches learning targets to assessment methods.

A Maplewood Richmond Heights Elementary School student pauses after reading her exhibit copy to a teacher for feedback.

You may wonder why an assessment plan should include selected/constructed response tests, extended written response tests, or personal communication assessments when performance assessment is a good match for measuring most of the school museum achievement targets, particularly the product target. Why not simply use teamwork, research, exhibit design, and label copy rubrics (provided in later chapters) to assess student learning in the school museum project?

You certainly could. But using varied assessments will give you a more complete picture of student learning and allow you to see student achievement in each target area with more clarity. Perhaps a student is performing well with research, writing, and exhibit design but doesn't have a firm handle on important content. Rubric scores alone may not reveal this knowledge gap. Selected/constructed response tests and extended written response tests may be better at pointing out student misunderstanding.

Students study one focus question in depth, but they are also responsible for learning all museum content once the exhibition is installed. Consider developing a pre-assessment to establish baseline information about student understanding of the museum topic. You might create a selected/constructed response test using statements of expected student learning, or you might develop an extended written response test using the focus questions. If you create two versions of your test, you will have a post-assessment as well, and you can use results to gauge your students' growth.

Ultimately, you want evidence that students achieved *all* learning targets, so an array of assessment data will be useful. You will also want evidence of student learning during the project; for this, ongoing, student-involved assessment is essential.

Figure 4.2
Plan for Matching Learning Targets to Assessments

Learning Target	Classroom Assessment Method			
	Selected/Constructed Response Test	Extended Written Response Test	Performance Assessment	Personal Communication
Knowledge: Student knows core facts and concepts. School museum target *Knowledge:* Student is able to answer each of the focus questions in the school museum (student as content expert).	Good match for assessing core facts and concepts. School museum ideas Create test based on statements of expected student learning for each exhibit.	Good match for assessing understanding of relationships among elements of knowledge. School museum ideas Create a pre-test and post-test for exhibit focus questions.	Not a good match for assessing knowledge alone, but a good match for use of knowledge in context. School museum ideas Use exhibit design rubric, content trait.	Good match but time-consuming process. School museum ideas Listen to docent tour, ask questions, evaluate answers, and infer understanding.
Reasoning: Student uses knowledge to reason and solve problems. The student may induce, deduce, analyze, compare, classify, evaluate, or synthesize. School museum target *Reasoning:* Student uses multiple resources to find relevant information and synthesizes research notes to answer research and focus questions (student as researcher).	Good match for assessing basic patterns of reasoning around core facts and concepts. School museum ideas Create test based on statements of expected student learning for each exhibit, making sure to include reasoning items.	Good match if certain that writing skill will not interfere with the students' ability to reason and solve problems. School museum ideas Create a pre-test and post-test for exhibit focus questions.	Good match if the product or performance requires and assesses reasoning proficiency. School museum ideas Use research rubric to evaluate students' work.	Good match. Ask students to "think aloud," or ask follow-up questions to probe reasoning. School museum ideas Listen to docent tour, ask questions, evaluate answers, and infer understanding.
Performance skills: Student uses knowledge and reasoning while performing skillfully.	Not a good match. Cannot infer through these methods that the student has the skill being assessed. May be able to assess understanding of prerequisite performance skills.		Good match. Can observe and evaluate skills as they are being performed in the task.	Good match if oral communication proficiency is being assessed.

Figure 4.2   (continued)

Plan for Matching Learning Targets to Assessments

Learning Target	Classroom Assessment Method			
	Selected/Constructed Response Test	Extended Written Response Test	Performance Assessment	Personal Communication
School museum targets *Performance skills:* Student interacts effectively with museum visitors, explaining exhibit content and actively engaging visitors in learning (student as skilled communicator). *Performance skills:* Student works effectively on a team (student as team player).	Not a good match. Cannot infer through these methods that the student has the skill being assessed. May be able to assess understanding of prerequisite performance skills.		School museum ideas Use teacher-developed oral communication rubric for docent presentation. Use teamwork rubric to evaluate students' work.	School museum ideas Listen to docent tour, ask questions, evaluate answers, and infer understanding.
Products: Student creates quality products that require use of knowledge, reasoning, and performance skills. School museum targets *Products:* Student writes appropriate label copy that describes exhibit artifacts and answers research and focus questions (student as writer). *Products:* Student designs appealing, effective, informative displays that answer focus questions and engage visitors (student as exhibit designer).	Not a good match. Cannot evaluate the quality of student products with these methods. May be able to assess prerequisite understandings.	Good match if writing proficiency is being assessed. School museum ideas Not appropriate for these targets in this project.	Good match. Can assess student performance in creating the product and can assess the quality of the product. School museum ideas Use exhibit design and label copy rubrics to evaluate students' work.	Not a good match. Can assess knowledge of procedures and knowledge of attributes of quality products, but cannot assess the quality of the product itself.

Adapted from Classroom Assessment for Student Learning (p. 100), by R. Stiggins, J. Arter, J. Chappuis, and S. Chappuis, 2004, Portland, OR: Assessment Training Institute. Copyright 2004 by Assessment Training Institute. Adapted with permission. Copyright 2004 by Kid Curators. Reprinted with permission.

Figure 4.3
Grading Plan

Learning Target	Assessment Method
Knowledge: Student is able to answer each of the focus questions in the school museum (student as content expert).	• Selected/constructed response test based on the statements of expected student learning for all exhibits • Extended written response test (pre-test and post-test) with all museum focus questions as prompts • Exhibit design rubric score for content trait
Reasoning: Student uses multiple resources to find relevant information and synthesizes research notes to answer research and focus questions (student as researcher).	• Research rubric score • Research write-up and graphic organizer of research findings
Performance skills: Student interacts effectively with museum visitors, explaining exhibit content and actively engaging visitors in learning (student as skilled communicator).	• Teacher-developed oral communication rubric for docent presentation
Performance skills: Student works effectively on a team (student as team player).	• Teamwork rubric score
Products: Student writes appropriate label copy that describes exhibit artifacts and answers research and focus questions (student as writer).	• Label copy rubric score
Products: Student designs appealing, effective, informative displays that answer focus questions and engage visitors (student as exhibit designer).	• Exhibit design rubric score

Based on learning target categories in Stiggins, Arter, Chappuis, and Chappuis (2004). Copyright 2004 by Kid Curators. Reprinted with permission.

Involving Students in the Assessment Process

Typically, when we think of an assessment, we think of a test, rubric, or graded assignment. We rarely think of reflective writing, descriptive feedback, or goal setting. These student-involved activities are assessments; they just aren't *summative* assessments. They don't measure what the student *has* learned; they measure what the student *is* learning—in time to actually use the results to improve achievement. This is *formative* assessment.

Summative assessments help students answer the question "What did I learn?" Formative assessments help students answer the question "What can I do to learn more?" Teachers have used formative assessments for years to improve instruction. But "What can I do to learn more?" is a student question. It implies that students will be involved in assessing their own progress and using the results to guide their learning. A simple example of formative, student-involved assessment is the use of rubrics to self-assess writing. When students use scoring rubrics that describe the traits of high-quality writing, self-assessment is more than an evaluative exercise; it also promotes greater learning. Students can use descriptive rubrics both to evaluate their draft work and to set improvement goals.

The skillful use of ongoing, student-involved assessment that promotes learning can serve as a strong motivator for students, as mentioned in Chapter 1. By participating in the assessment process—the development of assessments, tracking of progress, and communication of results—students better understand how to be successful (Stiggins et al., 2004). This insight increases their confidence, motivates their learning, and builds their sense of responsibility for attaining learning targets, which are all keys to improving student achievement.

Using student-involved formative assessment strategies will enlist students as partners and promote learning. Widespread use will also have a positive effect on summative assessment results—on your classroom assessments (grading plan) and perhaps even on your standardized test scores. Black and Wiliam (1998) synthesized more than 250 studies concerning the effect of high-quality formative assessment on student learning, and they found that using formative assessment can produce significant learning gains for all students. In particular, it "helps low achievers more than other students and so reduces the range of achievement while raising achievement overall" (p. 141).

Developing Strategies for Student-Involved Assessment

Providing opportunities for formative, student-involved assessment will improve student performance. Activities such as goal setting, evaluating anonymous work, self-assessing, and revision will show students how close they are to hitting their learning targets. This ongoing evaluation *is* assessment, although it is not what we typically think of when we hear the word.

The student-involved instructional strategies in this chapter are designed to engage students in ongoing assessment and bring their performances closer to the ideal. Many of the strategies are adapted from Stiggins and colleagues (2004), Arter and Chappuis (2001), and Arter and McTighe (2001). These strategies are a natural part of the school museum process and easy to incorporate. Appendix B provides an overview of student-involved assessment strategies that occur at different phases in the school museum project. Although you probably won't use all of these strategies, you should provide students with many opportunities to examine, evaluate, and adjust their work in progress.

Envisioning High-Quality Work

Giving your students a clear learning target means more than simply clarifying the language of the target; it also means ensuring that students know what high-quality work for that target looks like. Students need to understand the criteria by which they will be judged. If they can use those criteria to study models of strong and weak work, they are more likely to effectively apply the desired traits to their own upcoming work.

Help students brainstorm features of high-quality work. (See Stiggins and colleagues, 2004, pp. 232–234.) One way to encourage understanding of a learning target is to ask students to brainstorm characteristics of high-quality work for that target. For instance, in preparation for a museum project, students will discuss the types of museums they have visited and the exhibits that they found most and least intriguing (see Chapter 5). They will also assess displays in a professional museum, a local retail store, or in their school hallways (see Chapter 6). They will use these experiences to brainstorm the characteristics of high-quality exhibits—traits that they may be evaluated on during the school museum project. By defining the characteristics of good exhibits, students develop a vision of what high-quality work looks like.

Consider asking students to brainstorm features of high-quality work for other phases of the project such as teamwork, research, and writing; doing so helps students define excellence for each target. When their ideas are incorporated into the school museum rubrics, students develop a deeper understanding of the work that is expected of them.

Suggested rubrics for teamwork, research, exhibit design, and label copy are provided in later chapters, but just like the learning targets, the rubrics are useful only if students understand what they mean. They should be clear, descriptive tools that define quality performances. If you teach younger students, you will need to modify the language of the rubrics so that your students understand them. Alternatively, you could have your students develop their own rubrics based on an analysis of strong and weak work for each target. Consider having them develop three levels of quality for each trait, as in the teacher rubrics in this book.

Evaluate samples of high-quality and low-quality work. (See Stiggins and colleagues, 2004, pp. 234–235.) Rubrics help students understand the criteria for high-quality work, but alone they may not be sufficient to show students what high-quality work looks like. Wiggins (1993) suggests that students also need "models of excellence"—examples of good work that students can emulate (p. 49). Similarly, examples of weak work can help students understand when criteria are not met.

Before students begin their own work, have them use the school museum rubrics to evaluate strong and weak samples of work. For example, before students write label copy, they could rate samples of label copy using the rubric as a scoring guide. This task will strengthen their understanding of what high-quality work looks like and will give them practice using the rubric. You can use professional samples (museum copy, exhibit pictures, and so on) or students' work from a previous project (such samples should always be anonymous).

Randall Elementary School students, about to practice interacting with visitors, get pointers from their teacher on how to give good descriptive feedback to one another.

Achieving High-Quality Work

Students must understand the school museum learning targets and associated rubrics, but if they are to attain the vision of high-quality work, they must also recognize the "tangible differences between current performance and hoped-for performance" (Wiggins, 1993, p. 182). Descriptive feedback and self-assessment can show students how their work measures up to the standard—to the criteria for high-quality work that are outlined in the rubrics. Once students understand their strengths and weaknesses, they can set goals, improve their work through revision, reflect on their achievements, and achieve high quality work.

Offer students descriptive feedback. According to Marzano, Pickering, and Pollock (2001), providing feedback is one of the nine instructional strategies that has a high probability of enhancing student achievement. The authors found that "simply telling students that their answer on a test is right or wrong has a negative effect on achievement.

Providing students with the correct answer has a moderate effect. . . . The best feedback appears to involve an explanation as to what is accurate and what is inaccurate in terms of student responses" (p. 96). The authors explain that feedback is more effective when it is specific to criteria because it allows students to see where they stand in relationship to the target. Similarly, Wiggins (1993) suggests that feedback is useful when students see it as "user-friendly information on how I am doing and how, *specifically,* I might improve what I am doing" (p. 182).

Students self-assess their progress during the school museum project and set goals for future work.

Throughout the project, students should receive descriptive feedback about what they are doing well and what they can do to improve their performance.

Positive feedback is a valuable teaching tool and a motivator. In fact, before you share any corrective feedback with your students, consider showing them all the ways in which their work *already* reflects the criteria. Stiggins and colleagues (2004) suggest that you provide students with descriptive feedback while they are learning:

> Descriptive feedback should reflect student strengths and weaknesses with respect to the specific learning target(s) they are trying to hit in a given assignment. Feedback is most effective when it identifies what students are doing right, as well as what they need to work on next. One way to think of this is "stars and stairs"—What did the learner accomplish? What are next steps? All learners, especially struggling ones, need to know that they did something right, and our job as teachers is to find it and label it for them, before launching into what they need to improve. (p. 43)

The school museum project is a long-term, in-depth process. Students will be encouraged to persist if they see what they are doing right. Occasionally students can use the rubrics for the sole purpose of identifying what they are doing well. You can do the same—use the rubrics to point out the excellent work that students are doing.

Students also need feedback to learn how to improve their work. However, if students are told *everything* that needs improvement in their work at once, they may feel overwhelmed. Selective feedback is more useful, especially if it is centered on the elements of quality that are the current focus of instruction (perhaps one trait from the rubric). If feedback is limited to a reasonable number of improvement suggestions—the amount the student can act on independently—it is even more likely that the student will be motivated to persist. (See Stiggins and colleagues, 2004, p. 236.)

Teach students self-assessment techniques. In addition to receiving descriptive feedback from their teachers or peers, students can identify their own strengths and areas for improvement. Such self-reflection is an important habit and necessary if work is to improve over time. As students self-assess, they should examine their strengths and weaknesses to set goals for continued work.

Stiggins and colleagues (2004, pp. 236–239) discuss an assessment process for students called the three-minute conference. In this process, students self-assess their work, meet with their teacher to discuss strengths and weaknesses, and come up with an improvement plan. Students use rubrics to evaluate their work prior to the conference. Figure 4.4 on p. 56 shows a sample form for the three-minute conference.

After your students identify the strengths and weaknesses present in their work, ask them to meet with you to discuss their progress. Your feedback will be more meaningful to them if they have had time for self-reflection. Students can take their own feelings and your opinions into account as they develop specific, targeted ideas for improvement. (For more information on setting goals, see Stiggins and colleagues, 2004, pp. 45, 236–239, 240.)

Provide students with opportunities for revision. Descriptive feedback and self-assessment give students a clear sense of how well their performance meets the criteria, but to improve their work they need the opportunity to revise it. Wiggins (1998) believes that "authentic work involves achieving high-quality results, and such success depends on multiple opportunities to perform" (p. 34). Obviously, there is no point in setting improvement goals if there aren't opportunities to revise work and improve performance.

Students are often impatient with the revision process; they expect to create acceptable results on their first attempt. Consider modeling revision for students so that they can see how draft work can be improved (research notes, label copy, exhibit design, and the like). Students then learn about the full process of creating and revising, replete with the inherent struggles, decisions, and dilemmas. When students

Figure 4.4
Three-Minute Conference Form

NAME: _____   DATE: _____

Work being assessed: _____

MY OPINION

My strengths: _____

_____

What I think I need to work on: _____

_____

MY TEACHER'S OPINION

Strengths: _____

_____

Work on: _____

_____

MY PLAN

What I will do now: _____

_____

Next time I will ask for feedback from _____

_____

Adapted from Classroom Assessment for Student Learning *(p. 238), by R. Stiggins, J. Arter, J. Chappuis, and S. Chappuis, 2004, Portland, OR: Assessment Training Institute. Copyright 2004 by Assessment Training Institute. Adapted with permission.*

encounter their own difficulties, they will remember their teacher's similar experience and regard their struggles as a natural part of the process.

Guided practice is another valuable strategy for teaching students how to improve their own work through revision. Guided practice allows your students to become familiar with one or more traits from the rubric and allows you to informally assess their proficiency with the skill. Students can work in teams or alone to practice revision using anonymous class work samples or samples from professional museums (exhibits or label copy). Focusing on a single trait makes the task more manageable. The following suggestion from Stiggins and colleagues (2004) works well in the school museum project:

> Ask students to brainstorm advice for the (anonymous) author on how to improve the work. Then ask students, in pairs, to revise the work using their own advice. Or ask students to write a letter to the creator of the sample, suggesting how to make it stronger for the aspect of quality discussed. (p. 45)

Students should use the revision skills they observed and practiced to improve their own work, one trait at a time. (For more ideas about revision, see Arter and Chappuis, 2001; Arter and McTighe, 2001, pp. 88–90; Stiggins and colleagues, 2004, p. 240.)

If students are having difficulty with revision, they may need more information about how they can improve the quality of their work in relationship to specific rubric traits. Each rubric trait could be the focus of a short lesson that teaches students one aspect of quality at a time. (A sample mini-lesson on teamwork is provided in Chapter 5.) Consider designing mini-lessons based on the rubric traits. For example, the research rubric focuses on clarifying research questions and locating, summarizing, analyzing, and synthesizing information (Chapter 7); the exhibit design rubric focuses on organization, content, presentation, and effect (Chapter 8); the label copy rubric focuses on organization, relevance, voice, presentation, and grammar (Chapter 9). Mini-lessons focus on one trait and help students understand how all traits come together in the final product.

Consider modeling the thinking process for students in your mini-lesson, being careful to show where they may get stuck and how they can move beyond these predictable pitfalls. (See Arter and Chappuis, 2001; Arter and McTighe, 2001, p. 93; Stiggins and colleagues, 2004, p. 239.) This activity can be quite useful as students begin work on research, writing, or exhibit design.

Provide students with opportunities for reflection. Portfolios can be wonderful tools for encouraging self-assessment and showing students the result of their improvement efforts. As your students produce work throughout the project, they review their own progress toward the learning targets and select work samples that show their growth and mastery. As students select and explain examples of work that demonstrate mastery of the learning targets, they develop confidence in their emerging proficiency as a content expert, researcher, writer, team player, and exhibit designer. Using the rubrics, they write reflective pieces to explain how they developed proficiency toward the targets, presenting their work samples as evidence of their growth.

As a complement to this data, students can write reflective entries that describe the problems they encountered along the way and the strategies they used to solve them; how they arrived at the answers to their research and focus questions; or how they have grown in their proficiency. Consider asking students to complete the following reflective writing prompt as a way to summarize their growth over time: "I have become a better researcher [writer, team player, designer] this year. I used to . . . , but now I . . ." (Stiggins et al., 2004, p. 45).

Reflective writing need not be restricted to portfolio entries. A learning log or journal can be a useful tool that gives students additional chances to self-assess their progress. Barell (2003, p. 85) offers numerous examples of open-ended prompts for thinking journals, including the following writing stems:

- I wonder . . .
- What fascinates me here is . . .
- This is important because . . .
- This reminds me of . . .
- What is the meaning of . . . ?
- I do not understand . . .
- The big idea here is . . .
- What puzzles me is . . .
- I am changing my mind about . . .
- My goal for this week/month/semester is . . . , and here's how I intend to achieve it . . .

Reflective writing not only provides students with an opportunity for self-assessment; it provides you with insight into the learning successes and challenges of your students.

Summary

Determining what students actually learned in the school museum project is a key accountability issue. A high-quality assessment plan features clear learning targets and appropriate assessment methods. An assessment framework for your school museum project should include summative and formative components, as well as opportunities for ongoing, student-involved assessment. When students monitor their own work in progress, they are motivated to excel and reach the learning targets.

Part 2 The Process

5

Introducing the Museum Project

More than eighty 5th grade students are seated on the floor of the multi-purpose room at Bayside Middle School. Teacher Jane Elizabeth Marko asks them to close their eyes and visualize the room filled with museum exhibits that they have created: "It's opening night, and you are a proud museum staff member greeting visitors. Everyone is impressed with your work. People walk from exhibit to exhibit saying things like, 'Awesome,' 'Interesting,' 'I didn't know that.' Take a minute and try to imagine what those visitors see. Now open your eyes and describe what you saw." Excitedly, hands go up. Another teacher, Manon Gatford, steps in. Capitalizing on student enthusiasm, she emphasizes the magnitude of the task, careful to assure students that they can do it if they take their work seriously and work together. Teacher Stephen Schneider describes the upcoming activities, encouraging students to think creatively and critically. Finally, teacher Chuck Gilbert explains the importance of research and how necessary it is for students to know and understand the content they will present to their visitors.

Introducing the museum project is the first step of the eight-step instructional process outlined in the remainder of this book. Figure 5.1 on pp. 64–65 provides a graphic overview of the instructional process with key questions for each step.

Figure 5.1
Instructional Process Overview

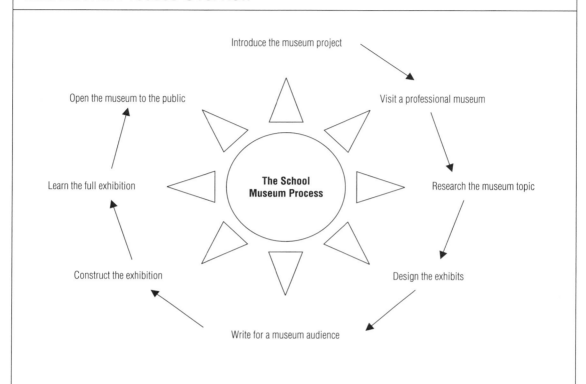

Step	Key Questions
Introduce the museum project	• What is our job? • What is a museum? • How will we work as a team? • What do visitors know and wonder about our topic?
Visit a professional museum	• What are the characteristics of high-quality exhibits? • What criteria will we use for our exhibits?
Research the museum topic	• What are our research questions? • Where will we locate information? • How will we summarize information as we take notes? • How will we analyze information to answer our research questions? • How will we synthesize information to answer our focus question? • What is our big idea? • What is our story line for visitor learning?

Figure 5.1 *(continued)*
Instructional Process Overview

Step	Key Questions
Design the exhibits	• What will we use to tell our story? • How do we get visitors to experience our story? • What will our completed exhibit look like? • Will our exhibit work?
Write for a museum audience	• Does the content and order of our exhibit labels help visitors understand our big idea? • Is our writing relevant and useful to the visitor? • Is the tone of our writing clear and consistent? • Does the visual quality, organization, and structure of our text make it easy to read? • Is the text in our exhibit grammatically correct?
Construct the exhibition	• How do we organize for construction? • How are we working as a team? • How will we install our exhibit?
Learn the full exhibition	• How can the completed exhibit be used as a teaching tool? • How can we engage visitors with our exhibit? • When will we take school groups on tours of our museum? • How will we learn about the other exhibits in our museum? • What did we learn?
Open the museum to the public	• What roles will we play on opening night? • What activities will we have during our opening night event? • How will we advertise our event? • What is our schedule for opening night? • How will we dismantle our museum? • How will we celebrate our accomplishments?

Copyright 2001 by Kid Curators. Reprinted with permission.

There are many tools for the instructional process; teachers should select those that are most appropriate for their situation. The teacher rubric in Figure 5.2 on pp. 66–67 describes three levels of quality for the instructional process. This rubric may help your team reflect on your project as it unfolds. Consider reviewing the rubric traits periodically during the school museum project and, if necessary, set goals for improvement.

Figure 5.2
Instructional Process Rubric

Note the performance level that is most descriptive of how the school museum instructional process is unfolding. If necessary, set goals for improving the quality of your instructional process.

Trait	Excellent	Progressing	Needs Improvement
Planning	Each step in the school museum process is planned in advance of instruction. Teachers understand, refer to, and incorporate the key questions for each step of the process as they plan the project (see Figure 5.1) and as instruction unfolds. Teachers understand the traits of high-quality teamwork, research, exhibit design, and label copy. They teach students about these traits and frequently refer to them throughout instruction.	Most of the steps in the school museum process are planned in advance of instruction. Teachers incorporate the key questions for each step of the process as they plan the project (see Figure 5.1), but once instruction is underway they rarely use the questions to focus students' work. Teachers understand the traits of high-quality teamwork, research, exhibit design, and label copy. They teach students about these traits at the outset of the project but seldom refer to them during the project.	The steps in the school museum process are not adequately planned in advance of instruction. Teachers understand the key questions for each step of the process (see Figure 5.1) but don't incorporate them in planning or actual instruction. Teachers superficially cover the traits of high-quality teamwork, research, exhibit design, and label copy during initial instruction but don't refer to them during the project.
Revision	Throughout the project, teachers reflect on students' work, assessment data, and their own impressions of the strengths and weaknesses of the project, and they adjust their instructional plans accordingly. Teachers plan mini-lessons in advance of instruction. They incorporate additional mini-lessons during the project when it becomes apparent that students need more support to develop their teamwork, research, writing, design, construction, or communication skills. Teachers monitor alignment of the learning targets, assessments, and instruction as the project unfolds and changes from its initial inception.	Teachers occasionally reflect on students' work and their own impressions of the strengths and weaknesses of the project, and they adjust their instructional plans accordingly. However, there isn't a systematic or consistent way in which teachers engage in this reflective work, and they do not consider assessment data. Teachers plan mini-lessons in advance of instruction. They don't incorporate additional mini-lessons during the project when it becomes apparent that students need more support to develop their teamwork, research, writing, design, construction, or communication skills. In planning the project, teachers align the learning targets, assessments, and instruction. When unpredictable changes occur as the project unfolds, teachers sometimes don't take the time for realignment.	Teachers rarely reflect on students' work and their own impressions of the strengths and weaknesses of the project. They do not consider assessment data. Rather, they devote their time to logistical issues or planning the next phase of the project. Teachers plan some mini-lessons in advance of instruction. They don't provide enough support for students to adequately develop their teamwork, research, writing, design, construction, or communication skills. Teachers don't carefully align the learning targets, assessments, and instruction when they plan the project or when changes occur as the project unfolds.
Teaching	Teachers effectively guide student teams as they produce high-quality research, label copy, and exhibits.	Teachers guide student teams as they produce research, label copy, and exhibits. They sometimes focus on production of high-quality work, but other times they sacrifice this focus to meet project deadlines.	Teachers urge student teams to complete their research, label copy, and exhibits but don't effectively guide this work.

Figure 5.2   *(continued)*
Instructional Process Rubric

Trait	Excellent	Progressing	Needs Improvement
Teaching	Teachers effectively manage the unfolding and sometimes changing project time line. They oversee the effective use of time among student teams.	Teachers effectively manage the unfolding and sometimes changing project time line. But sometimes student teams waste time by being off task or being confused about what they are to do.	When unexpected changes occur within the project, time line adjustments are made haphazardly and are not well communicated among teachers or to students. Sometimes student teams waste time by being off task or being confused about what they are to do.
	Teachers use the school museum project as an opportunity for student learning and skill development. They don't maintain a narrow focus on completion of the project in and of itself.	In planning the project, teachers view the school museum as an opportunity for student learning and skill development. Once the project is underway, however, there are times when the completion of the project becomes the priority.	Teachers view the school museum project as an end in itself and often prioritize the completion of the project above the opportunity for student learning and skill development.
	As the project unfolds, teachers help students see connections between their new knowledge and old knowledge.	As the project unfolds, teachers sometimes help students see the connections between their new knowledge and old knowledge. Sometimes they don't take the time to do this due to project deadlines.	Teachers rarely help students see the connections between their new knowledge and old knowledge. Instead, they are focused on project completion.
	Instructional plans include adequate time for student-involved formative assessment. For all learning targets, students have the opportunity to monitor the quality of their work in production and watch their performance improve.	Instructional plans include some time for student-involved formative assessment but not enough for students to be able to monitor the quality of their work in production.	Because there isn't a clear time line for the project, there is no way to know whether students will have adequate opportunities for student-involved formative assessment.
Student collaboration	Teachers systematically arrange for and promote interdependent collaboration among students.	Teachers promote collaboration among students, but sometimes independent work overwhelms collaborative work. The interdependence of team members isn't evident.	Teachers place students on teams, but students function independently. Rarely do they share their work and collaboratively develop a coherent answer to their focus question. Team members aren't interdependent.
	Teachers monitor student teamwork and ensure that roles are assigned within teams. Each team has a student leader who keeps the group focused and on task. This role may be rotated among students, but there is always a capable student in this role.	Teachers emphasize the importance of teamwork and ensure that roles are assigned within teams. Teamwork isn't closely monitored throughout the project, and there are times when teams don't have effective student leadership.	Teachers emphasize the importance of teamwork but don't adequately ensure that roles are assigned within teams. Teamwork isn't monitored throughout the project, and many teams don't have effective student leadership.

How Do You Begin the Project?

Now that you have completed the groundwork for your school museum, you are ready to begin the project with your students. You have defined the museum topic, big idea, story line, focus questions, statements of expected student learning, research questions, and an assessment plan. Students have already heard about the upcoming project—perhaps they have answered know and wonder questions about the topic. You are now set for the official kickoff.

To formally introduce the museum project to his students, Mike Moore of Waunakee Intermediate School asked them to describe the best museums and exhibits they had ever seen. After students shared their experiences, Moore told them that a new World War II museum was opening in Waunakee: "I asked them if they would like to visit that museum, and they were thrilled. I asked them if other kids would [want to] visit it, and they all agreed. You should have seen their faces when I told them they were the curators of the museum!"

In planning your introduction, consider these questions that student curators might ask (with some prompting from their teacher):

- What is our job?
- What is a museum?
- How will we work as a team?
- What do visitors know and wonder about our museum topic?

The introduction to the school museum should address these questions and present the learning expectations for the project.

Many teachers give students a broad overview of the topic to build their background knowledge and put their upcoming exhibit work into perspective. You might present this overview to the class through mini-lessons, learning centers, books, or videos on the topic. For instance, to present an overview to their 6th grade students, Elmwood Elementary School teachers Pat Morrissey, Susan Bush, and Jim Slonac created a one-page background sheet for each focus question and used the sheets in combination with a history video series.

Another way to provide students with an overview of the museum topic involves concept mapping. In the know and wonder activity described in Chapter 3, students created a visual web of information that represented what they knew and wondered about the museum topic. Once the museum topic has been officially introduced, students might create a new concept map reflective of the emerging project.

Figure 5.3 shows how this visual organizer might look. The museum topic is at the center of the concept map, focus questions are the first spokes out, and additional layers of detail come from the know and wonder chart, the museum overview, front-end evaluation data from visitors (explained later in this chapter), and students' ongoing research findings. The concept map is a powerful way to represent knowledge and integrate information. It also reminds students that they will be working on one part of a larger project.

Figure 5.3
Concept Map for School Museum Project

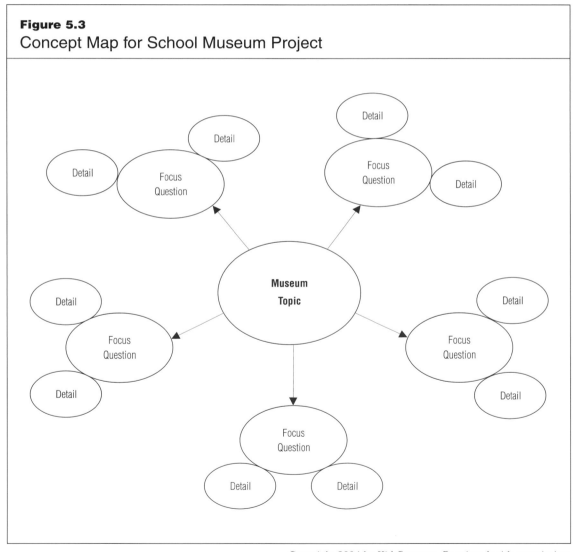

What Is Our Job?

Your students will play two roles in the school museum project. They will be young curators creating a school museum, and they will be students working to meet learning goals and earn good grades. The "What is our job?" question is relevant for each role.

As creators of a school museum, students have a specific mission to develop an interesting and informative exhibition for their school and community. This mission can be presented in an engaging way by using a strategy common in problem-based learning: giving students a loosely defined, real-world problem or challenge that serves as the context for upcoming instruction. Students "meet the problem" (Torp & Sage, 1998) in a role other than that of student; in our case, as museum curators and exhibit developers.

Consider presenting students with their "job" as it might be presented to an exhibit design firm—with a memo from a potential client, such as the sample in Figure 5.4. In fact, curators or exhibit designers in your community might be willing to help you create a letter inspired by a story about one of their exhibitions. For example, the fictitious letter in Figure 5.4 was inspired by a true story from the Veterans Museum of Wisconsin. A semi-permanent exhibition at the museum was set in motion after the director visited the British Museum of Military History, where he saw an Enigma machine (a machine used by the German armed forces to encrypt messages). He was so intrigued with this artifact that he returned from the trip eager to secure an Enigma machine for his museum. The director brainstormed ideas with museum curators. They felt that an exhibition about Enigma machines would be too narrow, but a story about communication and intelligence could be compelling, especially if it involved the contributions of Wisconsin veterans. They employed the services of a design firm to shape their emerging idea and created the exhibition *Uncovering the Enemy: Military Intelligence in the 20th Century*.

Even though the request in this letter is very specific and won't match your school museum topic, it serves as an example of how you might explain the museum design problem to your students. You could introduce the problem when you begin instruction or even earlier, before the know and wonder activity described in Chapter 3. If your letter includes a description of why the exhibition is significant and what it should accomplish, it can be used throughout the instructional process to maintain student focus on satisfying the needs of the "client."

Figure 5.4
Exhibition Request Letter

Museum of World History
Anywhere, USA 12345

January 5, 2004

Dalke Exhibit Design
456 Center Avenue
Your City, MO 23456

Dear Curators and Exhibit Designers:

I would like to contract with your exhibit development team to create a new exhibition for our museum. While visiting the British Museum of Military History, I saw a German Enigma machine on display. I was intrigued by this machine and its elaborate system of translating messages to code. I was especially interested in the story of the team of scientists who broke the cipher. Many speculate that this contribution had an important influence on the outcome of the war.

The year 2005 will mark the 60th anniversary of the end of World War II, and many visitors have been asking for exhibits that highlight unique contributions of those who did not fight in combat. Our visitor survey results indicate an interest in exploring the role of intelligence during wartime. We would like your design team to use the German Enigma machine as a centerpiece of an exhibition that explores the themes of intelligence and communication and highlights the contributions of individual veterans.

I look forward to reviewing your proposal.

Sincerely,

I. M. History
Executive Director of the Museum of World History

Requests, in the form of letters or personal visits from authentic sources, are also great ways for students to "meet the problem." These requests may come from a local museum or other community organization or from an individual. Beginning the project with a request adds credibility, as students will work to fulfill the needs of a client; it also creates an opportunity for community collaboration. You may want to contact individuals or community groups that might be interested in presenting a request to students. Consider these possible requests:

• The mayor requests a museum about your community.
• The school board requests a museum about the history of your school.
• The zoo requests an exhibition about native snake species.
• The historical society requests a black history museum.
• The Jewish Community Center requests an exhibition for Holocaust Remembrance Day.

The young curators in your classroom have another important job—to meet state standards and earn good grades. This aspect of the museum project also requires careful presentation. Be sure to review the learning targets and grading plan for the school museum with your students (see Figure 4.3 on p. 50).

What Is a Museum?

Now that students are clear about their job, they face another fundamental question: "What is a museum?" Although students are likely to have some answers to this question, the following activities will sharpen their ideas.

Types and Purposes of Museums

Teachers report that simply brainstorming types and purposes of museums can be a real eye-opener for students regardless of their experience. One teacher was surprised to find out how many museums her students had visited, whereas another was surprised by how few—but even this teacher noted that many students who had never visited an art or history museum had been to hands-on science centers and zoos.

Another teacher said that this exercise not only expanded his students' definition of *museum*, but his own as well. When students were asked, "What museums have you visited?" they came up with a variety of different types—science centers, zoos, historical homes, nature

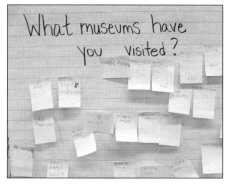 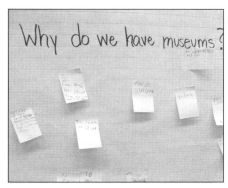

As students list the museums that they have heard of or visited, they quickly recognize that there are many types and purposes of museums.

centers, botanical gardens, art museums, history museums, and specialty museums. Upon reflection, this teacher realized that many of these informal learning environments provided useful models for school museum exhibits. This experience sparked his personal interest in visiting a wider range of museums and led to new ideas for his next school museum project.

Discussion of similarities and differences among types of museums can lead to another question: "What are the purposes of museums?" When students in Kim Kuchler's 2nd grade class at Maplewood Richmond Heights Elementary School answered this question, their ideas included "to help us learn," "to look at stuff," and "to explore." Many museums also collect, classify, preserve, and display artifacts. Answers such as "to look at stuff" seem to imply this purpose, and teachers can make the connection more explicit.

Objects and Images in Museums

Discussion about the types and purposes of museums can lead to a significant observation—all museum exhibits use objects to engage their visitors. This is true for museums as different as SciTrek: The Science and Technology Museum of Atlanta, a hands-on science center, and the Milwaukee Public Museum, a natural history museum. SciTrek is an "experience" museum; its aim is to make abstract physical science concepts more accessible to the public through hands-on activities. It does not have an extensive collection of artifacts; preservation is not part of its mission. In contrast, the Milwaukee Public Museum has an enormous collection. Some of their artifacts, objects, and images are displayed in realistic dioramas that capture the imagination of visitors. According to Peter Haydock, the senior director of education and public programs, less than 2 percent of the collection is displayed on the museum floor! Part of the collection may be displayed in future public exhibitions, loaned to other institutions, or used by visiting researchers, but some objects will never be seen by visitors—they are being preserved for the public trust. The Milwaukee Public Museum and SciTrek are very different museums, but they both use objects and images to create experiences for visitors. (See Chapter 8 for more about the use of objects and images.)

Organization of Museum Displays

Early in the process, even before they visit a professional museum, students will benefit from learning about how museums organize material. Ann Clifton, a museum educator and curator from the Samuel Cupples House and the Saint Louis University Museum of Art, visited Maplewood Richmond Heights Elementary School and spoke to 3rd graders about the roles of curators and docents. The class discussed different curator responsibilities—deciding what goes in a museum, how to display it, how to teach the public about an exhibition, and how to attract museum guests. Students curated their own tabletop museum by arranging images of objects that "belonged together"—historical artifacts, paintings, Egyptian mummies, and sports memorabilia. Students were able to see connections among different, seemingly unrelated objects and arrange them to tell a story. The 3rd graders quickly understood how objects can be grouped effectively to communicate a message.

Peg Koetsch, founder of the program Museum-in-Progress, uses a similar technique in an activity she calls "Thinking like a Curator." Koetsch assembles a variety of postcards, each representing a work of art that uses different media, style, subject, and compositional technique. She gives students one postcard image to study and asks them to imagine it as an artifact in their museum collection. Koetsch places a postcard in the center of a table and asks if anyone has an artifact that connects to it. If so, they place their postcard near the original image and explain how it is connected. For example, a student might say that both of the works of art are painted with oils, illustrate people, or use symmetry as a compositional technique. Students continue making these connections until the images are grouped together. As they analyze and critique this "exhibition," students move images to make stronger connections and identify group themes. Then students give this exhibition a title reflective of its overarching concept.

You might ask students in your classroom to think like curators and have them group "artifacts" from a previous instructional unit. For example, an elementary science unit on sound might have artifacts such as wire coils that simulate sound waves, varying lengths of tubing that create different pitched sounds, student-created musical instruments, and other samples of students' work. Students could group these artifacts to tell the story of sound. As you review their grouping decisions, ask students what their visitors will learn about sound and have them explain how the artifacts, together, communicate that message. Perhaps this introductory activity will result in a classroom mini-museum, a worthy culminating activity for an instructional unit.

How Will We Work as a Team?

Interdependent collaboration within and among exhibit teams is one of the many learning opportunities in a school museum project, as discussed in Chapter 2. It is also one of the great challenges. Students develop collaborative skills—and make mistakes—as they engage in the work of creating a school museum. Yet there is no better way to learn how to be a team player than by doing the real and often difficult work of collaboration. Fortunately, some strategies can make this work easier for teachers and students.

Students at Elmwood Elementary School work together to construct their exhibit.

Creating Teams

One of the best ways to organize students for successful teamwork is to carefully establish teams. Creating a diverse group will promote productive collaboration; try to balance teams in terms of gender, ability, and leadership skill. To also allow student choice, teachers at Elmwood Elementary School in New Berlin, Wisconsin, asked students to list their top three areas of interest from 11 focus questions and to list one exhibit they did not want to work on (if there was one). When teachers assembled teams, they considered their students' input.

Team size is another significant factor. Teams of three to four students are ideal, whereas larger teams add to the complexity of managing work and negotiating group dynamics. A group's large size can add undue burden to students who are learning how to function as effective team members. In fact, Marzano, Pickering, and Pollock (2001) note that group size of six members or more can actually have a nega- tive effect on achievement (p. 88).

Clarifying Roles and Responsibilities

Teams function best when responsibility is shared by all members and when each member's role is clear. Even in adult meetings, team- work quickly deteriorates when there is uncertainty about who is lead- ing the discussion, preparing the minutes, or following up on particular items. Similarly, it is important for students to clarify their roles and responsibilities as team members. As a class, decide who will assume responsibility for each role; roles can be rotated. Examples of team roles include the following:

• *Leader:* Sets direction for the team, makes sure team members understand what they have to do, gets things going, and keeps things moving.
• *Timekeeper:* Informs team members when time limits are approaching and helps keep the team on task.
• *Recorder:* Makes note of team decisions.

These roles can be modified for the age of your students and the composition of your teams. Pat Morrissey, a 6th grade teacher at Elmwood Elementary School, thought that her teams could function more efficiently with defined roles, so she created a list of roles appro- priate for her students. She presented the roles to students and asked them to make assignments within their teams. Once roles were in place, students immediately noticed an improvement in their performance, as reflected in their following comments:

> Sometimes people can get off task but we have jobs, and one of the per- son's jobs is to keep people on task. That's been working pretty good lately. We're getting a lot accomplished.

> I think [roles] help because we all have certain responsibilities to do and that helps the rest of the group. If we didn't have assigned roles . . . we wouldn't get anything done.

Regardless of their roles, all students are responsible for being good team members. The rubric in Figure 5.5 on p. 78 lists traits of good team- work in a school museum project. You may present students with this rubric, or you may prefer to have students develop their own. Most students have been part of a group project or cooperative learning activity and can describe what it was like when teamwork went well and when it didn't. Those experiences will help them think about ways to ensure that their team functions effectively. A rubric clarifies the teamwork learning target and makes it easier for students to assess their skills and set goals for improvement.

Communicating Teamwork Expectations

The student responsibilities outlined in the teamwork rubric communicate expectations for teamwork behavior. You will also need to communicate the expectation that students will take responsibility for these behaviors, their work, and the smooth functioning of their team. Harmin (1994) identifies the "intelligence call up" strategy as one way to "advance students' ability to handle their lives responsibly, wisely" (p. 118). This strategy asks students to stop when faced with a problem and consider what would be the intelligent thing to do. The strategy communicates confidence in students—"You are smart and know what to do"—and encourages them to be part of the solution. When an individual or team confronts this question, they take responsibility for their work: "We are having a problem. What should we do? Let's brainstorm some solutions." This strategy can go a long way to promote student independence and shared responsibility within the classroom.

Foyne Mahaffey, a 1st and 2nd grade multi-age teacher at Lake Bluff Elementary School in Shorewood, Wisconsin, instructs students to "ask three before me." Students know to ask three peers for clarification or direction before they go to Mahaffey with their concern. This simple rule communicates great confidence in the students and distributes responsibility for learning among the members of the classroom community.

Another way students can demonstrate responsibility in the school museum project is by putting forth their best effort. Research shows that not all students realize the importance of effort.

> Although it might seem obvious to adults—particularly successful ones—
> that effort pays off in terms of enhanced achievement, not all students are
> aware of this. In fact, studies have demonstrated that some students are
> not aware of the fact that the effort they put into a task has a direct effect
> on their success relative to the task. . . . The implication here is that
> teachers should explain and exemplify the "effort belief" to students.
> (Marzano, Pickering, & Pollock, 2001, p. 50)

Figure 5.5
Rubric for Teamwork

Trait	Always 5	Usually 4	Sometimes 3	Seldom 2	Never 1
Productive: I came to class prepared, started work right away, and stayed on task.					
Responsible: I completed my work and performed my team role.					
Contributing: I shared information with my teammates and asked for their feedback.					
Communicative: I listened to my teammates when they had something to say, and I gave my opinion when decisions were to be made.					
Collaborative: I asked my teammates to share their ideas and opinions, and I helped the group make important decisions.					

Teamwork score: _____

How could you improve? List one or two goals for upcoming work.

_____

_____

_____

_____

To help students see the relationship between effort and achievement, you might ask them to use the rubric shown in Figure 5.6 to track their effort and connect it to improved achievement.

Improving Teamwork Skills

Once your project is underway, you may want to develop mini-lessons to improve teamwork. Consider using Harmin's (1994) "task and team skill group" strategy, in which a small group works at a task and simultaneously practices an interpersonal skill (p. 114). The strategy consists of four steps and takes about 45 minutes to complete, so you

Figure 5.6
Effort and Achievement Rubrics

Scale: 4 = excellent; 3 = good; 2 = needs improvement; 1 = unacceptable

A: Effort Rubric	**B: Achievement Rubric**
4 I worked on the task until it was completed. I pushed myself to continue working on the task even when difficulties arose or a solution was not immediately evident. I viewed difficulties that arose as opportunities to strengthen my understanding.	4 I exceeded the objectives of the task or lesson.
3 I worked on the task until it was completed. I pushed myself to continue working on the task even when difficulties arose or a solution was not immediately evident.	3 I met the objectives of the task or lesson.
2 I put some effort into the task, but I stopped working when difficulties arose.	2 I met a few of the objectives of the task or lesson, but did not meet others.
1 I put very little effort into the task.	1 I did not meet the objectives of the task or lesson.

From Classroom Instruction That Works *(p. 52), by R. J. Marzano, D. J. Pickering, and J. E. Pollock, 2001, Alexandria, VA: Association for Supervision and Curriculum Development. Copyright 2001 by McREL. Reprinted with permission.*

will want to use it when you suspect it will save time in the long run by reducing existing or anticipated problems.

Step 1 is to assign students an individual task. The following are examples of school museum tasks:

• Draft a letter to someone who has firsthand knowledge of your research or focus question and request information or an interview.

• Create a preliminary drawing of your exhibit.

• Design one interactive component for your exhibit.

Step 2 is to assign a group product for the task. The following examples correspond to the tasks listed in Step 1:

• a final version of a letter that incorporates the best of individual drafts

• a drawing of the exhibit that incorporates the best of individual preliminary drawings

• an interactive component for the exhibit that incorporates the best of individual ideas

Students work in their exhibit teams to create this product, and they practice one or two specific teamwork skills that need to be developed, such as listening closely to one another, returning to work when they notice they are off task, disagreeing respectfully, paraphrasing, or sharing opinions honestly. Students should consider *how* they might demonstrate these skills. For example, if they plan to practice listening closely to one another, they should first brainstorm what they might say or do when they are not listening well and when they are listening well.

A teacher at Maplewood Richmond Heights Elementary School prepares her students for their work on exhibit teams.

Step 3 is to review the teamwork skill as soon as teams have developed their product. Ask students to do some reflective writing: "When did you or someone in your group practice the target skill? What would you do next time you have a chance to practice this skill? In what other situations in your life could you use this skill?" After students have reflected on the lesson, engage in a large-group discussion about these questions.

Step 4 is to review the task and the work of each small group.

Teamwork is a critical feature of the school museum project and something that students practice in each step of the process. Be sure to make time for students to regularly reflect on their teamwork skills and to work on improving them.

What Do Visitors Know and Wonder About Our Topic?

Early in the conceptual phase of exhibit development, museum professionals engage visitors in a process known as front-end evaluation. Through focus groups or interviews, evaluators find out what visitors know about the topic, what is of interest to them, and their expectations for the upcoming exhibition. Museum professionals consider front-end evaluation a vital tool to "uncover, examine, and then set aside our own preconceptions about visitors so that we can see and understand more clearly what they know, believe, and are interested in" (Dierking & Pollock, 1998).

Liz Forrestal, an exhibit developer at the Saint Louis Zoo, considers front-end evaluation critical in the early stages of exhibit development. By talking to audiences before designing the Monsanto Insectarium, evaluators found out that many visitors didn't know the difference between an insect and other kinds of small invertebrates. In response, the exhibit team designed *Am I an Insect?* to address visitor misconceptions. Insects, spiders, and millipedes are on display, each accompanied by a flip door with the question "Am I an insect?" After examining the live animal in each display case, the visitor opens the flip door to find the answer and explanation. Forrestal also wants to know how the visitor feels about the exhibit topic. Front-end evaluation for the Monsanto Insectarium revealed that many visitors simply do not like insects. This negative perception prompted exhibit developers to create displays that highlight the importance of insects.

Student curators can conduct front-end evaluations for their exhibit by asking their parents, other adults, or their peers about the museum topic or a specific focus area. Questions they might ask include the following:

- What do you know about this area?
- What do you wonder about this area?
- What about this area interests you?

Exhibit and evaluation consultant Beverly Serrell (1996) suggests other questions that your student curators might consider, such as "What would you expect to do, see, find out about in this exhibit?" (p. 97) and "What comes to mind when you see or think about X?" (p. 137).

Asking prospective visitors for input can build anticipation for the coming school museum. Waunakee Intermediate School teacher Mike Moore wanted to ensure that his school's World War II Museum would generate curiosity among students and visitors. As students explored the wartime contributions of men and women from different cultural groups, Moore encouraged them to conduct front-end evaluation. Students asked their parents what they knew and wondered about the Tuskegee Airmen, Navajo code talkers, and other groups.

When students ask their parents about their exhibit topic, they involve them in school activities and encourage interest in the upcoming museum. The conversation may also broaden students' background knowledge and provide new ideas for their displays.

Summary

Introducing the school museum may include a dramatic kickoff event to capture students' imagination and build excitement for the project. The introduction should clarify the learning expectations for students and anticipate their questions about project work. Providing background knowledge about the museum topic is usually necessary before research and exhibit design begin. Background knowledge helps students put the project in perspective and shows how upcoming exhibit work connects to a larger whole.

Students are better able to imagine their exhibition when they understand the different types and purposes of museums and how museum displays rely on objects and images to engage visitors. To create their exhibit, students will need to work together as a team. Each step of the school museum process is made easier when students understand their teamwork roles and responsibilities. As they begin to develop their exhibition, student teams conduct front-end evaluation, which provides an opportunity for parental involvement.

6

Visiting a Professional Museum

Fifth graders from Maple Avenue Elementary School are at the Milwaukee Public Museum to study displays before they begin working on their school museum project. Curator Dawn Scher Thomae leads them to the *What Is a Butterfly?* exhibit and asks what they see. One student notices a large butterfly image; another is curious about the spider inside a case. They move to another exhibit, *Cultural Expressions*. One student is impressed with a Chinese ceramic vase; another is interested in a rotating case of butterflies. Scher Thomae asks students to describe the visual qualities of these exhibits, the things that drew their attention. She listens and then shares her thoughts. She describes the spider case as the only three-dimensional item in an otherwise two-dimensional exhibit; students recognize that objects make an exhibit more interesting. Scher Thomae tells students that the large butterfly image provides a visual focal point for that exhibit—it's the first thing that visitors see. She points to empty space on the exhibit panel and asks students why nothing is there. They aren't sure. Then she explains—the eye tires quickly when there is too much text or visual stimulation. Students see exhibit qualities they have never noticed before. They will make more observations later, when they explore the museum in their small groups.

A visit to a local museum gives students the chance to observe and identify the qualities of good exhibits—knowledge they will later use with their own designs. Even without the benefit of a curator's insight, students learn a great deal by analyzing professional exhibits.

Sometimes it is not possible to visit a museum. If this is the case, students can study displays in shopping malls, grocery stores, retail windows, or libraries, or even take a virtual tour of a museum online. But if you can, it is better to visit a professional museum with your students, and better still if the museum is one that mirrors the school museum you are about to create—a science center if you are creating a science exhibition or a history museum if your exhibition is about history. One way or another, students should see good models of professional work; the experience will provide them with a deeper understanding of the characteristics of high-quality exhibits.

Hunt for High-Quality Exhibits

Although most students have visited a museum, they have probably not done so for the purpose of analyzing displays. During the museum visit, student teams can search for high-quality exhibits and describe their characteristics, using an observation guide such as the one shown in Figure 6.1.

Some teachers ask students to find an example of one high-quality exhibit and one poor-quality exhibit and to complete an observation guide for each exhibit. Bad examples can provide just as much insight as good examples. As students explain why an exhibit didn't work— why it was not engaging, informative, well organized, creative, or instructive—they learn what to avoid in their museum design. Photographs taken at the museum will later help students describe their selected exhibits. Teachers may want to visit the museum on their own to take photos for future classroom use. (Museums have different policies on photographing exhibits, so be sure to consult museum staff before taking pictures.)

Before the museum visit, students can practice using the observation guide by examining exhibit photographs from professional museums (many of which are available at museum Web sites) or by describing exhibits they have visited in the past. At the museum, your full class can examine several carefully selected exhibits together before teams study exhibits on their own. The curator, teacher, or an adult chaperone can generate discussion among students using questions from the observation guide.

Figure 6.1

Observation Guide for Museum Visit

Find an exhibit that you think is excellent and explain why. We will use your ideas to generate our list of criteria for high-quality exhibits.

Name: _____   **Date:** _____

Museum: _____   **Exhibit:** _____

Description of Exhibit: _____

How does this exhibit . . .

Engage?

Does the exhibit capture and maintain your interest? How?

Inform?

Does the exhibit tell a simple but important story? What is it?

What points of view are represented?

Organize information?

What objects and images are used to tell the story?

How is text used to interpret these objects and images?

How are different ideas connected to one another?

Show creativity?

Does the exhibit arouse your curiosity and imagination? How?

What are some of the clever, original, or unique display techniques used in this exhibit?

Teach?

Does the exhibit teach you something new or help you see something in a new light? How?

What should we remember about this exhibit as we begin our project?

If students visit the museum later in the project, after research and before developing display ideas, consider the following alternatives to the observation guide. These ideas relate to material found in Chapter 8.

• Find the big idea of a museum exhibition.
• Find the story line of a museum exhibition.
• Explain the visitor learning goals (knowledge, affect, and action) for an exhibit.
• Find the ways in which the exhibit involves the visitor.
• List the objects and images that tell the exhibit story and explain why you think they were selected.
• Brainstorm ways to adapt an exhibit.
• Find an exhibit that relates to visitors' personal experiences.
• Find exhibits with visual, auditory, tactile, or kinesthetic enhancements.
• Come up with three display ideas that could be modified using inexpensive materials.

Students from Maple Avenue Elementary School prepare to review exhibits at a professional museum.

In addition to (or instead of) the observation guide, students may simply take "field notes" as they tour the museum. With their learning logs in hand, they jot notes about what they see, where they see it, and their reactions. They can look for the use of lighting and color, the varying sizes of text, and the kinds of objects and images displayed. Later they can analyze their notes and use them to answer this question: "What did you notice at the professional museum that could help us as we create our school museum?" (For more on field notes, see Barell, 2003, pp. 92–96.)

Chat with a Curator

A behind-the-scenes tour or curator "chat" can enhance a museum visit and motivate students. Depending on the museum's staffing capabilities, this chat could be several minutes or several hours long. If you are unable to set up a personal meeting, you may be able to arrange a virtual chat or tour, provided that your school has the appropriate technology.

In her chat with 5th graders, Milwaukee Public Museum curator Dawn Scher Thomae asked, "What comes to mind when you think about museums?" She used several of the students' ideas to explain museum work and the role of curators. This lead to a discussion of what makes a good exhibit and the process of exhibit design at the museum. Scher Thomae also presented a brief history of museums, explaining that they started informally more than 100 years ago with the collections of the wealthy put on display for their friends and family. Students were excited to meet a museum curator and learn from a professional in the field before they began their own museum work.

Dawn Scher Thomae, a curator at the Milwaukee Public Museum, talks to 5th grade students.

Follow-Up to the Museum Visit

Shortly after the museum visit, give students the opportunity to process what they have learned. Students saw models of good (and probably bad) exhibit design at the museum; they should reflect on this new knowledge and relate it to their upcoming exhibit work. Students also had a chance to practice their teamwork skills, maybe for the first time during the project; they should reflect on this experience as well.

Creating and Using the Exhibit Design Rubric

Back in the classroom, student teams share their photographs (if available) of the high-quality exhibits they selected during their museum visit and describe the features of quality that prompted them to select those exhibits. When team presentations are complete, the class may create its own trait-specific exhibit design rubric that the teacher can add to or modify as needed. Alternatively, the teacher may introduce the rubric in Figure 8.1 (on pp. 116–117) and ask students to identify the features of quality in the rubric that they just described in their presentations. By doing this, students will see that they are already familiar with some of the rubric traits and will understand that they are about to learn more about the features of high-quality exhibit design. Throughout the project, students can look for good and bad display examples and present them to the class, using the exhibit design rubric to evaluate them. When students use the rubric to evaluate exhibits, they come to better understand the rubric traits and can later apply this understanding to their own exhibit design.

Evaluating Teamwork

After the museum visit, students can self-evaluate their teamwork efforts and share specific examples of good teamwork behavior, linked to rubric traits. As a leader of this discussion, be ready to point out what students already know about teamwork (when they share good examples) and what they will learn during the project (when they share poor examples). After this assessment activity, consider preparing a mini-lesson to allow students to practice teamwork skills that need additional work. (See Chapter 5 for a sample mini-lesson on teamwork.)

Summary

A focused field trip to a professional museum is an important component of the school museum project. By carefully examining effective and ineffective professional displays, students learn the traits of high-quality exhibits and use that knowledge to shape their upcoming exhibit work. Careful preparation for this visit—including the development of an observation guide, modeling the use of that guide, and clarifying the purpose of the museum visit for students and chaperones—is critical to the success of the visit. Some museum curators may be willing to meet with the students while on site, which adds another dimension to the experience. The museum visit provides opportunities for students to build teamwork skills and develop a vision of high-quality work for their exhibit designs.

7

Researching the Museum Topic

Theresa grew up listening to her grandmother's firsthand account of the Holocaust, and she tells the 6th grade Holocaust exhibit team at Elmwood Elementary School about the hardships her grandmother faced as a prisoner in Dachau. She also explains how prisoners supported one another by sharing food, telling stories to keep their minds stimulated, and talking about what they would do when—not if—they were liberated.

Students thank their guest speaker for her visit. As soon as Theresa leaves, they begin talking about display ideas, eager to create an exhibit that captures all they have learned. Just days ago, the Holocaust seemed an obscure topic to these students, but now after hearing of the plight of Theresa's grandmother, history seems real to them. Teacher Pat Morrissey makes the most of students' enthusiasm and reminds them that more research is needed before they are ready for exhibit design. She explains that although Theresa was a valuable source of information, students' research questions about Nazism, Hitler, and concentration camps need more complete answers. "Your exhibit is going to be great," Morrissey tells her students, "but only if you truly understand your topic, which involves additional research. You will be able to create whatever you want the audience to see from what you learned, but you need to go through the complete research process first." The exhibit team members are initially disappointed—they wanted to begin their designs immediately—but they agree that more research will help them create an impressive exhibit. Morrissey walks away, pleased. She recognizes the sense of purpose the museum project provides, purpose that motivates student research.

Students cannot design an exhibit unless they know something about the subject matter. They are naturally excited about creating their school museum and are eager to get to the hands-on phase of the project. Exploit their enthusiasm now—during research (and as they write)—and require that they complete the foundational work before beginning design and construction. Students with early display ideas may draw them in a learning log or sketch pad, but exhibit development comes later, after students complete their research.

Although research is critical to every school museum project, no two projects approach it in quite the same way. Student research differs depending on a number of factors, including the grade level, whether a research curriculum is in place (if so, it can be integrated into the project), and the museum topic.

This chapter presents five basic research steps in a school museum project:

1. *Clarify research questions:* Focus areas of research.
2. *Locate information:* Use a variety of resources.
3. *Summarize information:* Take notes.
4. *Analyze information:* Examine notes to draw conclusions and answer research questions.
5. *Synthesize information:* Share information with teammates to answer focus question and write a big idea and story line.

The research rubric in Figure 7.1 on pp. 92–93 lists important components for each step.

Before work begins, consider asking students what they already know about research. Have they done research before? What steps did they take? What did they do at each step? Their research experiences may prompt more questions: What problems might researchers face if they don't understand the question? What is wrong with researchers using only one source of information? This discussion will help students understand the research process they are about to begin.

Teachers of very young students may present research information as a series of interactive classroom lessons, rather than require independent research. After students learn about the museum topic together, they form exhibit teams to design and construct displays from those lessons.

Clarifying Research Questions

If you planned the school museum project as outlined in Chapter 3, you have prepared exhibit focus questions for your topic, along with related statements of expected student learning, student research questions, and links to your academic standards. Additional questions may have surfaced during the front-end evaluation (Chapter 5); consider providing time during the first exhibit team session for students to refine and further develop their research questions.

Students at Maplewood Richmond Heights Elementary School use age-appropriate sources of information to research their museum topic.

Student teams must thoroughly understand their questions before they can successfully conduct research. If questions are too broad, students may not know how to begin research. For example, a 4th grade exhibit team from Browning Elementary School was given the research question "Where did immigrant groups settle?" For some students, such a broad question may need to be revised before it can provide direction for research. A "think aloud," modeled by the teacher, may help students make their questions more explicit:

> We are studying different cultural groups—specifically the Germans, Italians, and Irish. So, this research question wants me to find out where—in which cities—each group settled when it first came to Wisconsin. Where would I begin . . . maybe with one immigrant group? If I started with the Germans, for example, I could try to find out where they settled when they came to Wisconsin. Then I could move on to another cultural group. It may be easier to research this question: "Where in Wisconsin did many Germans, Irish, and Italians settle when they first arrived?"

Once students understand the meaning of their research questions, they are in a better position to find the information they need to answer these questions.

Figure 7.1

Rubric for Research

Trait	Excellent 5	Very Good 4	Adequate 3	Needs Improvement 2	Not Acceptable 1
Clarifying research questions: **I focused my research on questions I understood.**					
I understood my research questions before beginning my research.					
I wrote additional research questions based on the results of my front-end evaluation.					
I stayed focused on my research questions.					
Locating information: **I used a variety of appropriate information sources.**					
I identified sources of information that addressed my research questions.					
I gathered information using appropriate search strategies.					
I evaluated sources of information based on their accuracy and relevance.					
I sought additional information when necessary.					
I used multiple sources of information to answer my research questions, including primary and secondary source information when appropriate.					
Summarizing information: **I read and reviewed research, took notes on key points, and referenced my sources.**					
In my notes, I included key points and supportive facts related to my research questions.					
I cited references appropriately as I took notes.					
I wrote notes in my own words and didn't copy directly from the source unless I quoted.					
Analyzing information: **I used information from my research notes to draw conclusions about my research questions.**					
I drew conclusions about my research questions based on a thorough review of my notes.					
I evaluated how well my research conclusions answered my questions.					

Figure 7.1 *(continued)*

Rubric for Research

Trait	Excellent 5	Very Good 4	Adequate 3	Needs Improvement 2	Not Acceptable 1
I created a fully developed answer to my research questions, including specific facts or examples.					
I created a graphic organizer that represented the answer to my research questions.					
Synthesizing information: **My exhibit team reviewed the information for each research question and used it to answer our focus question.**					
We drew conclusions about our focus question based on a review of each team member's research findings.					
We evaluated how well our research conclusions answered our focus question.					
We created a fully developed answer to our focus question, including specific facts or examples.					
We created a graphic organizer that represented the answer to our focus question.					
We developed a big idea for our exhibit to help us decide what to include in our displays.					
We developed a story line of visitor learning goals for our exhibit.					
We presented our research findings to our classmates.					

Research score: _____

How could you improve? List one or two goals for upcoming work.

_____

_____

_____

_____

Locating Information

Students should use multiple and diverse sources of information to answer their research questions. In *The Research Workshop* (2001), teacher Paula Rogovin explains how she begins class research studies—by asking students what they already know about the topic. As students tell what they know, Rogovin asks them another question: "How did you learn that?"

> They may say they learned it from a parent, an uncle, a video, or a movie, or that they saw it somewhere. Some of the sources may be available to help us in the classroom. (p. 14)

Not all research information must come from nonfiction print material, which may be difficult to find for young researchers. Students and teachers should broaden their view of research material; by viewing "sources of information" and "research materials" synonymously, new possibilities open up.

During a planning meeting at Maplewood Richmond Heights Elementary School in Maplewood, Missouri, teachers were having difficulty finding age-appropriate resources for their 2nd graders. The following were the focus questions for their Communities Museum:

• How are urban, rural, and suburban communities alike and different?
• How do communities make decisions and rules?
• How do people live, work, and play in their community?
• Why do people move?
• How do changes in technology affect people's lives?
• How can a community deal with its problems, and how can people work to make the community a better place?

As teachers discussed their concerns about the lack of adequate age-appropriate print materials, one teacher suggested that they consider alternative sources of information. She had taken her students on a community walk that provided excellent information about their topic. A second teacher told of an invited guest who came to speak to students about their focus question. Another explained how a trade book sparked student conversation and interest in their topic. As one by one these teachers shared their stories, they realized that they were already using many sources of information appropriate for 2nd grade research. They left this meeting reassured; even without many print materials written at a 2nd grade level, there were sources of information for student research on their topic.

Consider using the question "How will we find out?" with your students (or with your teaching team) to create a web of information sources for your museum topic. For example, 3rd grade teachers from Lovejoy Elementary School in Alton, Illinois, generated a research web as they planned their school museum (see Figure 7.2 on p. 96).

Another planning tool for students (or teachers of young researchers) is presented in Figure 7.3 on p. 97. This table organizes research efforts by connecting information sources to specific exhibit research questions. Remind students that as they locate, gather, and review information, they should evaluate it in terms of accuracy and relevance to their question. Sometimes what was thought to be a helpful source of information is rejected, and the search begins anew.

Students can use information sources such as people, places, and trade books to research their topic. The following examples may generate useful ideas for your project and broaden the sources of information that your students access.

People

As students and teachers begin to locate information for research, they often ignore the most obvious and easily accessible resource available—people who have knowledge of the museum topic. Parents, other family members, community members, local authorities, and even friends are an underused research resource. The children themselves may be sources of information, as they often know something about the topic or know someone who does.

Students in Steve Walsh's class at Maplewood Richmond Heights Elementary School studied the focus question "Why do people move?" Walsh guided a whole-group activity in which his 2nd graders pooled their collective knowledge and used it as a source of information. Walsh divided the focus question into three research questions: (1) "What natural things attract people to a community?" (2) "What are some things that keep people in a community?" and (3) "What are some things that make people want to leave a community?" Students wrote their ideas on index cards, which Walsh collected and "accidentally" dropped on the floor. As he picked up the cards, students helped him sort them into the three categories. One card, for example, listed the word *trees*, which students identified as something that might attract people to a community.

Figure 7.2
Research Web

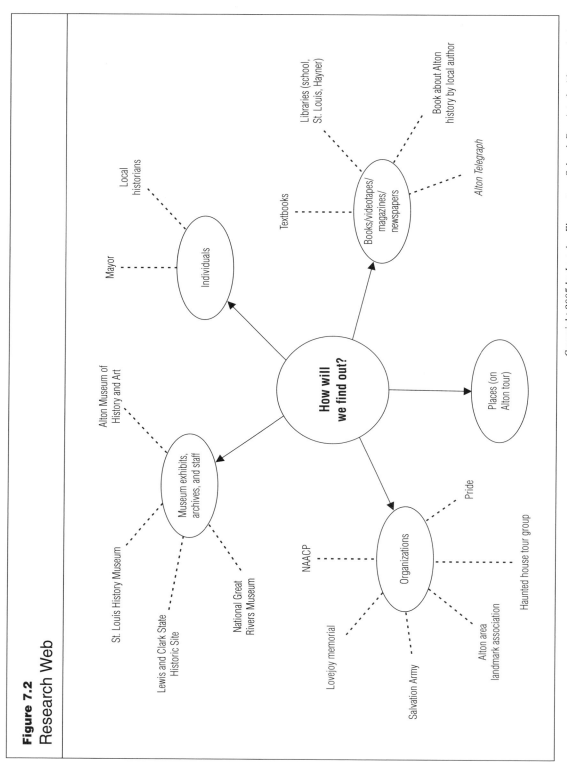

Figure 7.3
Research Planning Worksheet

Step 1: List your exhibit focus question and research questions.

Step 2: If you have your own questions in addition to the research questions for your exhibit, add them in Column 1.

Step 3: Decide who on the team will research each question. You may have more than one team member working on the same research question.

Step 4: Locate sources of information and include them in the appropriate column.

Step 5: Review the completed plan with your team to make sure all team members understand their jobs.

Focus Question:

Research Question	Who will research this question?	Where will you look for information?					
		Books	Magazines/ Newspapers	Videotapes/ DVDs/CDs	People	Places	Internet Sites

Copyright 2004 by Kid Curators. Reprinted with permission.

Job markets, economics, quality of education, and pollution were some student ideas about why people do or do not want to live in a particular community.

Walsh extended this activity by suggesting that students write letters to friends or family members who moved to other parts of the country and ask them why they left one community for another (see Figure 7.4 on p. 99). Students who received replies were eager to share their letters with their classmates. The personal stories gave students a much deeper understanding of why people move and what makes a community attractive.

Meeting people with firsthand experience about the museum topic can motivate students to learn more. For example, during the research phase of their Communities Museum, Lizzy Wolken's 2nd grade class gathered information about their focus question: "How are urban, rural, and suburban communities alike and different?" Because most students had no experience with rural life, they invited a guest speaker to visit their classroom—another teacher in the school who grew up on a farm in Iowa. She showed photographs of herself as a young girl and told students about farm chores such as milking cows and shearing sheep. Her stories about growing up on a farm, attending a country school, and living in a rural community gave students insight into the everyday differences among people who live in rural, urban, and suburban communities.

The library/media specialist at Elmwood Elementary School assists a 6th grader in locating information for her exhibit research.

In a museum project about 20th century history at Elmwood Elementary School, teacher Pat Morrissey described the day their guest speaker visited her 6th grade class as "one of our best days ever." Weeks before, Morrissey noticed an article in the local paper about World War II prisoner of war Arthur Lange, who had visited a nearby school to talk about his experiences. She shared the article with the exhibit team studying the land and sea battles of World War II. A student from the group invited Lange to the school. Students interviewed him in a private room and broadcast the interview into the 6th grade classrooms. Following the broadcast, Lange visited each classroom to answer follow-up questions.

Lange was happy to tell stories and even came with "artifacts"—identification tags; notes he wrote while in the prison camp dreaming of things he wanted to do upon his release; telegrams his mother received informing her that he was missing in action, then a prisoner of war of the German government, and finally released. These artifacts or copies of them might easily become part of an exhibit. But more important, information from the interview may prompt further research. For example, Lange told students that he was captured during the Battle of the Bulge. His story might inspire a host of additional research questions: When was the Battle of the Bulge? Why was it significant? What was the military strategy? The interview with Lange made the answers to these questions more relevant to the 6th grade students.

Firsthand accounts of history are fascinating to students; they make the subject matter come alive and put it in a personal context. Lange came to his interview with objects to talk about, but it could have worked the other way around—students could have presented him with objects and images in order to generate conversation. Some

Figure 7.4
Research Response Letter

April 11, 2004

Dear Charlotte,

You asked me several questions about why I live in Texas, whether I like living here, and what brought me here. These are interesting questions, and they make me think about my life, my friends, my family, and my career.

As you know, your daddy and I grew up in St. Louis. I went to college while I worked (and your daddy was in the Army for part of that time). I was very lucky to be interested in my job, and I realized I needed more education to better understand many things about engineering. School and education gave me many opportunities to make choices, and I had fun at work. Education is very, very important.

I first left St. Louis when I was 30 years old. I went to work at Carnegie Mellon University in Pittsburgh. It was very exciting, and I met new people and made new friends. I missed Grandma Nita and your daddy, but I had best friends in Pittsburgh, along with my family and old friends in St. Louis.

When I was 38, a company in San Antonio, Texas, offered me a different job. By this time, I had an interest in my career. A career is a little different than a job, because I had to learn more about more and more new things. I enjoy learning about stuff.

I am happy in Texas, but I think I could be happy in many places. I never knew a bluebonnet flower could be so pretty, or that I could play golf throughout the year. I have met some very interesting people, including people who live in other countries.

My daughters (your cousins) live in Chicago and San Antonio, and you, your mom and dad, Grandma Nita, and Emily and Ellen live in St. Louis. Sometimes I get sad and miss everybody, but most of the time I am very happy to have made the decisions about my work and about moving. My life is very interesting, and I get to visit all of my friends and family many times throughout the year.

I hope to see you all in the next few weeks when I visit St. Louis. Tell Uncle Dave and Peppy that I say hi.

Love,

Uncle Danny

Sixth graders from Elmwood Elementary School interview World War II veteran Arthur Lange.

companies provide program materials to support this process. Bi-Folkal Productions, for example, offers what it calls "reminiscence resources"—kits that can be used to invite the sharing of stories. Each kit has material designed to trigger memories from a particular time or topic. The *Remembering the Home Front* kit includes slides of Americans working and waiting for their loved ones to return from war. The kit also includes objects such as a hand-rolled bandage, military insignia, a Red Cross knitting project, and stickers of rationed items. These objects and photographs may encourage interviewees to tell stories about their experiences. (For more information on remembrance kits, visit www. bifolkal.org.)

An interview might corroborate information that students have already gathered or it might raise completely new areas for research. After students conduct an interview, ask them to review the transcript or their notes and list potential follow-up ideas for the exhibit—new research questions to explore and objects to include in their display. The value of an interview depends on how it is used as an information source.

There are probably many people within your community who could be information sources for student research. Teacher Paula Rogovin (2001) provides families with weekly updates about classroom research projects. She invites families to participate as interviewees or to send books, magazines, newspaper articles, and other materials that might support the research study. Rogovin describes past interviews and asks parents to talk to their children about them, and she encourages families to attend upcoming community visits, guest speaker events, and class activities. She also includes optional activities that parents can do with their children to reinforce classroom learning. For example, after an interview with Phil, a retired teacher living in a steel mill town, parents might try the following homework activity:

> Look at a map of Pennsylvania. Find Pittsburgh. Then look south of Pittsburgh for the Monongahela River, where there were many steel mills. Then find Clairton, where Phil was brought up. There were many coal mines in the same area. Talk to each other about why the steel mills and coal mines were in the same area. (p. 181)

A family discussion could lead to many research sources. Such activities encourage parental involvement and create interest in the research topic.

Places

People are not the only source of information for student research; community sites can also provide valuable research opportunities. Becky Pyatt, a 2nd grade teacher at Maplewood Richmond Heights Elementary School, took her students on a community bus tour to find answers to their focus question "How do people live, work, and play in their community?" Students observed many community sites, including schools, libraries, government buildings, department stores, pharmacies, and grocery stores.

They returned to school and created an ABC book to answer their focus question. As part of a collaborative effort with Webster University's Voices Across the River project, students met visiting author Kristen Joy Pratt, who is known for her ABC books *A Walk in the Rainforest* (1992) and *A Swim Through the Sea* (1994). Pratt taught students writing and illustration techniques, which they incorporated into their book exhibit. The exhibit was later displayed at the Missouri History Museum.

For their part in the Communities Museum, Kim Kuchler's 2nd graders studied the question "How do communities make decisions and rules?" Students visited city hall and met with the mayor, Mark Langston. They toured the mayor's office and the boardroom where city council meetings take place. Prior to this visit, students prepared a set of questions for Langston. They wanted to know more about the role of the mayor in city government and asked him such questions as, "What do you do every day?" "Do other people help you?" "Who makes the rules and laws of Maplewood?" and "Whom do you work for?"

Lizzy Wolken's 2nd graders learned about the features of suburban communities by taking field notes as they walked through the school's neighborhood. Their notes included observations about housing, transportation, and land use, and they were a valuable point of reference when students later studied urban and rural communities.

Trade Books

Dan Lyons's 2nd grade students at Maplewood Richmond Heights Elementary School answered the focus question "How do changes in technology affect people's lives?" Lyons found that students had a hard time with this question—they didn't have the historical perspective or personal experience to consider technological changes over time. To generate discussion, he introduced the book *If You Lived 100 Years Ago* by Ann McGovern (1999). This age-appropriate book made students curious about what life was like before television, automobiles, and indoor plumbing. Students were organized into research groups based on a particular technology. They researched the history of that technology and its influence on people's lifestyles. Students used the Internet and other resources to do this work, but the book provided the springboard for their research and also provided useful information for some groups.

In another classroom, teacher Suzanne Decker guided study of the focus question "How can a community deal with its problems, and how

For their Communities Museum, students at Maplewood Richmond Heights Elementary School created a three-dimensional ABC book.

can people work to make the community a better place?" Decker was not sure what to use as research material and found children's literature to be a good starting point. Students read and discussed *Fly Away Home* by Eve Bunting (1991), a story about a homeless boy and his father who live in an airport. Students also read books about homeless shelters. These stories presented the issue of homelessness to students in the context of a character's life and provided basic information about the reasons for, challenges of, and community responses to homelessness. One child wondered if there were homeless shelters in their community; another child said he thought there were and he would find out—his mother was a volunteer at the Salvation Army. The material provided an opportunity for students to ask questions that they could explore by contacting people they knew.

Students in Decker's class also studied people who have made a positive difference in the national or world community, including Martin Luther King Jr., Jimmy Carter, Florence Nightingale, Nelson Mandela, Mother Teresa, and Rachel Carson. Using books, the Internet, and library materials, students learned about the contributions of these influential people and developed an appreciation for the fact that individuals can do extraordinary things to make their communities better places.

This research led students to a new question: "What can *we* do to make our community a better place?" Using the categories of poverty, prejudice, war, and pollution, students brainstormed ways in which they could make their communities better. Students themselves were sources of information, and they incorporated their ideas into a video presentation. They suggested things that kids can do to improve their communities, such as bringing food to a pantry, donating clothes to a shelter, not judging people based on skin color, and recycling cans instead of throwing them away.

Primary and Secondary Sources

As students locate information, you may want to distinguish between primary and secondary sources, encouraging students to include both when possible. Primary sources are firsthand accounts of historical events created by witnesses or participants, whereas secondary sources are secondhand accounts that interpret or analyze the events. Examples of primary sources include diaries, autobiographies, government records, photographs, letters, newspapers from the era, interviews with participants, and historic objects. Secondary source information may be found in biographies, encyclopedias, history textbooks, media documentaries, interviews with scholars, and books and articles about the topic. (For more information and research tips, visit the research roadmap at http://www.nhd.org/researchroadmap.htm.)

Summarizing Information

Regardless of the sources of information that students use, they will need to summarize what they have learned. They will use their notes to answer their focus and research questions and develop their exhibits. Summarizing and note taking are instructional strategies known to improve student achievement. To be able to effectively summarize, students must understand information at a fairly deep level and make decisions about what information to keep, to delete, or to substitute (Marzano, Pickering, & Pollock, 2001).

Guided Note-Taking Lesson

A guided lesson will show students strategies for summarizing information. First, give students a general question related to your museum topic (for example, "What is a community?"). Then provide a single paragraph of research material for students to read. Modeling a "think-aloud" for students will show them how you make decisions about what to delete, substitute, and keep. Students can use a note-taking worksheet, such as the one shown in Figure 7.5 on p. 104, to record their results.

Students might practice taking notes using a lengthier piece, after which volunteers might share what they deleted, substituted, and retained from the original text. As an alternative guided practice activity, students might simply write key points from a single paragraph of research material. After several volunteers share what they wrote and

Figure 7.5
Research and Note-Taking Worksheet

Step 1: List the focus question for your exhibit and your research question. Use additional worksheets for additional research questions.

Step 2: Review your sources of information and write key points that answer your research question.

Step 3: As you take notes, be sure to cite your references. You may need to refer to these sources later.

Focus Question:

Research Question:

Information and Key Points	References

explain how they arrived at their key points, students discuss strategies for summarizing.

Note-Taking Techniques

If students don't have a formal process for taking notes, or if you would prefer a simpler process, consider the format shown in Figure 7.5. Otherwise, students should use the technique they are familiar with, such as the Cornell note-taking system. Many students use this method for taking notes while listening to lectures, reading research materials, viewing videos, or listening to CDs. (For more on the system and other study skills, see the Cornell University Center for Learning and Teaching Web site: http://www.clt.cornell.edu/campus/learn/ SSWorkshops/SKResources.html.)

Another effective note-taking strategy is the combination technique shown in Figure 7.6 on p. 106. Students create simple webs and add information in an outlining section. When the web is complete, students write a summary statement at the bottom of the note page.

As students summarize information and take notes, they should keep a detailed bibliography of their source material, including author names, titles, publication dates, page numbers, and Web site addresses. They may need to refer to a source of information later when they develop and design their exhibit content.

Analyzing Information

Students have read and summarized varied sources of information and are ready to answer their research questions. Developing a short written response to their research questions requires that they analyze their notes, prepare research conclusions, and evaluate how well they have answered their questions. This write-up may be useful as label copy (see Chapter 9), but it is not developed for this purpose. Rather, it is evidence of what students learned about their topic. Another way for students to present their research findings is in a graphic organizer (see Figure 7.7 on p. 107).

These products—the research write-up and the graphic organizer—will provide valuable assessment information about student understanding. Did students draw conclusions about their research questions based on a thorough review of their notes? Did they evaluate how well their research conclusions answered their questions? Is their answer fully developed, including specific facts or examples? Pat

Morrissey of Elmwood Elementary School had students submit a written summary of their research before moving on to exhibit design. This summary allowed her to evaluate whether students adequately understood their research findings—if not, she provided additional support as they continued the research process.

Students can use their research write-ups and graphic organizers to create several selected/constructed response test items for classmates. The test items should reflect the key findings related to their research questions. The process of generating test items requires that students review all their research information and select what is most important in relationship to their questions. Their decisions will provide you with insight into their learning—did their test reflect an understanding of important content? Good test items can be used later in the process to assess student understanding of the full exhibit.

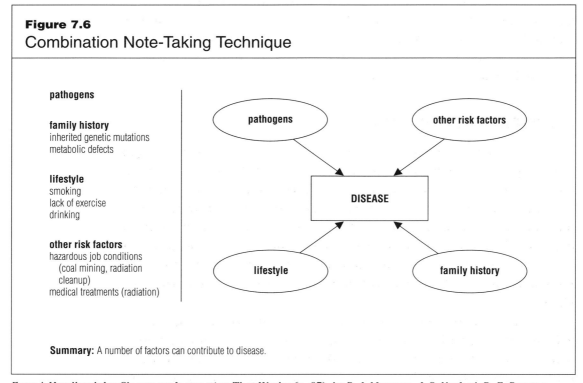

Figure 7.6
Combination Note-Taking Technique

pathogens

family history
inherited genetic mutations
metabolic defects

lifestyle
smoking
lack of exercise
drinking

other risk factors
hazardous job conditions
   (coal mining, radiation
   cleanup)
medical treatments (radiation)

Summary: A number of factors can contribute to disease.

From A Handbook for Classroom Instruction That Works *(p. 87), by R. J. Marzano, J. S. Norford, D. E. Paynter, D. J. Pickering, and B. B. Gaddy, 2001, Alexandria, VA: Association for Supervision and Curriculum Development. Copyright 2001 by McREL. Reprinted with permission.*

Figure 7.7
Graphic Organizer for Research Findings

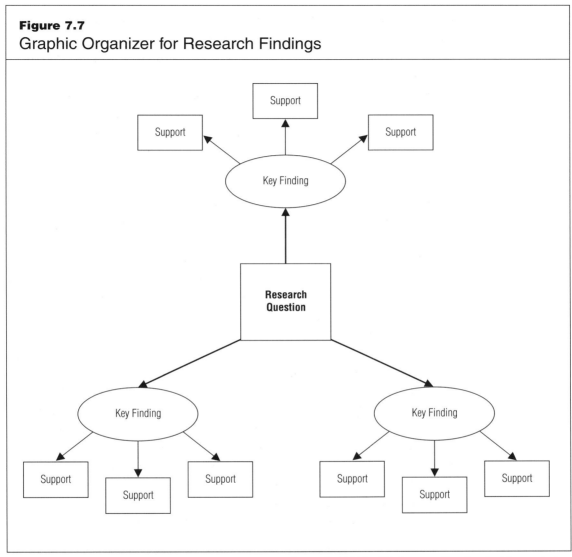

Synthesizing Information

When students have adequately answered their individual research questions, they share findings with exhibit team members. As a team, students develop a short written response to their focus question, similar to the write-up each student developed for research questions. This process forces students to step back from their independent research and integrate their collective knowledge. To adequately answer the focus question, students will have to listen carefully to one another, synthesize information, and evaluate the adequacy of their write-up.

Students transfer their collective information to a graphic organizer that combines the findings from individual research questions and connects them to the team's focus question (see Figure 7.8). This visual tool should help students synthesize and clarify the important ideas from their collective research. As students share their research, they begin to define the content of their displays, including the big idea and the "story worth telling" for their exhibit.

Creating a Big Idea for the Exhibit

The full exhibition has a big idea and story line; similarly, student exhibits have this cohesive structure. For example, the Seasons of Change Museum at St. Paul's Elementary School featured an exhibit gallery devoted to civil rights, which included a display about activism. A big idea such as "Activists fought to change policies and perceptions during the civil rights movement" summarizes student research findings and begins to define the content of the exhibit.

Developing exhibit big ideas serves a practical purpose as teams design their displays—it provides focus for upcoming decisions. After research, students will have many ideas about what to include in their exhibit, probably too many. They will be tempted to "tell" the visitor everything they know. This is a problem, as museum visitors don't spend a lot of time at any one exhibit. Student designers need to eliminate some of their ideas, and a big idea can assist in the winnowing process.

Professional exhibit designers also run into the problem of what to include in their displays. Exhibit developer Liz Forrestal worked with designers to create the Saint Louis Zoo's Monsanto Insectarium:

> It was tough because we had so many things we wanted to say. We came up with many more ideas than we could show. We had to remember our audience. We were excited, and we wanted to tell them everything. They may not want to hear it all! You have to make painful decisions.

So how did the team make those decisions? They went back to their big idea. Because the statement captured the important message of their exhibition—"Insects provide many benefits to humans"—it helped them determine which ideas to include and which to exclude.

Developing a Story Line for the Exhibit

When student designers are clear about their big idea, they are ready to answer the question "What do we want visitors to learn in our

Figure 7.8
Graphic Organizer for Synthesizing Research

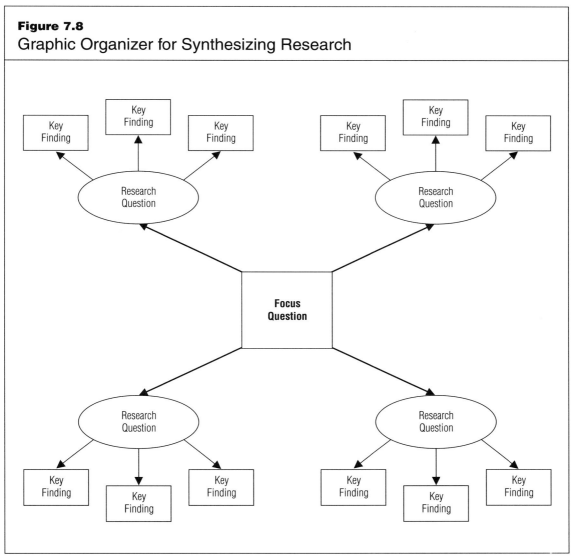

exhibit?" Every exhibit has components that address different aspects of its big idea. Together, these components tell the story of that exhibit. For example, an exhibit about activism might feature the following cohesive story line:

- Integration was a key issue in the civil rights movement.
- Martin Luther King Jr., Rosa Parks, and others were key figures in the civil rights movement.

An exhibit team from Elmwood Elementary School conducts history research to answer their focus question.

• Sit-ins, marches, and voter registration efforts were key strategies in fighting for equal rights.

• The Civil Rights Act was signed in 1964, but many struggles continue.

Notice that this sample story line is written as a series of visitor learning goals. Ultimately, exhibit developers create experiences for visitors—experiences that lead to new learning. But developers often begin by defining what they want visitors to learn as they experience the exhibit.

For example, the Saint Louis Science Center is renovating its ecology and environment gallery. During the early step of conceptual design, planners define learning goals for their audience. Exhibit developers identified numerous goals, including the following:

• The earth has been and continues to be shaped by geologic forces and processes.

• The earth's living things change through time.

• Scientists use tools and techniques to understand the earth's geology.

These goals form the story line of the exhibit and outline what the developers want visitors to learn.

Visitor goals need not be restricted to knowledge goals. Liz Forrestal of the Saint Louis Zoo explains that most of their exhibits include visitor goals on three levels: knowledge, feelings, and action. Designers use the three different types of goals to shape the experience of visitors:

• knowledge goals: information the visitor will learn
• affect goals: emotions the visitor will feel
• action goals: actions the visitor will take

A major learning goal for the Monsanto Insectarium is for visitors to develop an appreciation for insects. To monitor progress on this goal, museum professionals look at the results of surveys completed by visitors after they have seen the exhibition. The survey asks questions such as "How did you feel about insects before your visit to the Monsanto Insectarium today?" "Which do you think are important benefits that insects provide?" "What do you think is the coolest insect behavior?" "What do you feel about insects now that you have visited the Monsanto Insectarium?" and "What is your favorite animal in the Insectarium?"

An exhibit may also be designed to change visitor behavior. One of the galleries in the Saint Louis Zoo's education center includes an exhibit called *A Difference of One*. This interactive computer exhibit asks visitors to provide lifestyle information in answer to questions such as "Do you live in the city or country?" and "What is your primary mode of transportation?" The computer program uses this demographic information to search a database of hundreds of staff-generated environmental behaviors, and it chooses some that suit the visitor's lifestyle in five different areas: conserving resources, advocating for the environment, supporting wildlife and plants, improving environmental quality, and reducing solid waste. For instance, the computer program might suggest that "instead of paper towels, use rags, a towel, or a sponge whenever possible to reduce your use of disposable products." Similarly, students at Maplewood Richmond Heights Elementary School had an action-oriented visitor goal involving ways to make their community a better place to live.

The visitor learning goals—whether they are knowledge, affect, or action goals—should provide a general story line for the exhibit. The form in Figure 7.9 on p. 112 may be a useful organizing tool for student teams as they write visitor learning goals that will form their story line.

Presenting Research Findings

Students may use their graphic organizer, write-up, big idea, and story line to create a presentation that answers the focus question and highlights key findings from their research. Presenting research findings to classmates allows students to learn from one another and provides an opportunity for the presenting team to review their conclusions. In addition, if all students present their research, you can use the presentations to assess their content knowledge.

Figure 7.9
Exhibit Story Line Worksheet

Step 1: Fill out this worksheet with your exhibit team. List your exhibit focus question.

Step 2: Develop a big idea for your exhibit, a single statement that tells the visitor what your exhibit is about and why it is important—of all that could be explored, this is what will be explored.

Step 3: Write a story line for your exhibit—the key points that will be addressed in your exhibit. Together, these statements support your big idea and tell the story of your topic. They outline visitor learning goals—what you want visitors to learn, feel, or do as a result of visiting your exhibit.

Focus Question:

Big Idea:

Story Line for Visitor Learning:

Summary

Research is a critical part of the school museum process. Students cannot create informative exhibits unless they understand the subject matter. Although there will be much variation in the way research is conducted depending on the specific school museum project, all student research involves clarifying research questions, locating information, summarizing information, analyzing information, and synthesizing information. As students review their research findings, they write a big idea and story line for their exhibit to help them determine the content of their displays. A research rubric, written in language that students understand, will aid student self-assessment as well as teacher assessment of this learning target.

8

Designing the Exhibits

Randall Elementary School students Katy, Luke, and Jake are sitting on the floor near the spot where they will eventually install their *Wright Brothers* exhibit. They review their research organizer and talk about the story line for their exhibit. Then they brainstorm objects and images that they might use to tell this story. They know they won't use all their suggestions but want to create a long list of ideas they can narrow down. Jake takes notes for later review.

Their display ideas include a replica of the Wright brothers' experimental kites; pictures of aircraft they produced; a model of their first flying machine, a helicopter toy powered by rubber bands; and blueprints of different flying machine designs. The exhibit team also brainstorms ideas for auditory and hands-on experiences for their visitors. One student suggests that they create a listening station where visitors can press a button to hear something. A student remembers visiting a Web site that included a one-minute audio recording simulating the sound of a Wright brothers' aircraft; he wonders if they could feature the recording in their listening station. Shifting to ideas for hands-on experiences, another student suggests, "We could make a rubber-band powered toy that visitors could touch!"

Teacher Randy Kunkel asks students to complete their list of exhibit ideas and revisit their research organizer to see which ideas best support their story line for visitor learning. They start to narrow down their list and begin to sketch some possible exhibit designs.

When research is complete, students are ready to design their exhibit using the following guiding questions:

   • *What will we use to tell our story?* What objects and images will we select, and what presentation methods will we use to display them?
   • *How will we get visitors to experience our story?* How will we make our exhibit relevant to visitors? How can we engage their senses?
   • *What will our completed exhibit look like?* What inexpensive materials can we use to create our exhibit? How will we plan our space?
   • *Will our exhibit work?* Will visitors like our exhibit? Will it be a cohesive whole?

If students created an exhibit design rubric after their visit to a professional museum, they should refer to it as they craft their displays. Figure 8.1 on pp. 116–117 shows a trait-specific exhibit design rubric that may be used if students do not have their own. You can rewrite it in language appropriate for your grade level or revamp it into a checklist of items that your students should include in their exhibits.

What Will We Use to Tell Our Story?

Students have completed the hard work of research and have obtained enough knowledge to answer their focus question. They will use their story line for visitor learning to develop exhibit components for their display. First, they will need to think creatively and ask themselves a key question: "What objects and images would we need if we were to tell our story without words?"

Objects and Images

As Falk and Dierking (1992) point out, museums are different from other learning settings in one significant way:

> Museums are collections of things, some intrinsically valuable, others not. Objects are the essence of a museum. . . . The fact that a museum chooses to reach its goals primarily by displaying three-dimensional objects, while the others [institutionalized learning environments] invariably depend on words and two-dimensional pictures, distinguishes museums. (p. 77)

Objects are central to museum displays. Most professional museums obtain objects from their collections, purchase or borrow them from other organizations, or fabricate them. However acquired, objects are the visual devices that carry the story line of museum exhibitions.

Figure 8.1
Rubric for Exhibit Design

Trait	Excellent 5	Very Good 4	Adequate 3	Needs Improvement 2	Not Acceptable 1
Organization: **Information is well-organized for the visitor.**					
The orientation to the exhibit explains its purpose and layout.					
The big idea of the exhibit is clear.					
The story line (visitor learning goals) supports the big idea.					
The objects and images tell the exhibit story.					
Exhibit components make sense when viewed alone and together.					
The concluding message provides closure, reinforcement, or new insight for the visitor.					
Content: **Information is clear, complete, and accurate and generates interest in the subject.**					
The exhibit answers the focus question and develops the big idea.					
The exhibit presents information, generates curiosity, changes ideas or feelings about the topic, or motivates action.					
The story line (visitor learning goals) represents key points about the focus question and big idea.					
Various points of view are represented accurately.					
Information is accurate and facts are substantiated.					
Presentation: **The visual appeal, organization, and structure of the exhibit make visitor interpretation easy.**					
The type of exhibit (immersion, collection, dramatization, etc.) is a good match for the content.					
The graphic look and feel of the exhibit is a good match with the big idea and story line.					
Visual devices and label copy complement each other and, together, tell the story.					
There is no visual clutter in the exhibit.					

Figure 8.1 *(continued)*
Rubric for Exhibit Design

Trait	Excellent 5	Very Good 4	Adequate 3	Needs Improvement 2	Not Acceptable 1
Effect: Based on formative and summative evaluation data, the exhibit attracts visitors, holds their attention, and teaches the intended message.					
The exhibit is engaging; it attracts visitors and holds their attention.					
The visitor understands the big idea.					
The visitor finds personal meaning in the presentation; the exhibit makes connections to prior knowledge and is relevant to visitors' lives.					
The exhibit changes visitors' perspectives by enriching what they already know, teaching them something new, changing their ideas or feelings about the topic, or motivating them to act.					

Exhibit design score: _____

How could you improve? List one or two goals for upcoming work.

_____

_____

_____

_____

The *Sitting for Justice* exhibition at the National Museum of American History, for example, began with one powerful object: the F. W. Woolworth's lunch counter from Greensboro, North Carolina, where the Greensboro sit-in took place. In 1960, four black college students sat in this "whites only" diner and asked to be served. When refused, they remained seated and "ignited a youth-led movement to challenge injustice and racial prejudice" (Henderson & Kaeppler, 1997, p. 148). Curators believed that the lunch counter would be an effective device for interpreting aspects of the civil rights movement, and they were involved in a yearlong effort to acquire it. The acquisition of the lunch counter helped tell a compelling story:

> A marriage of idea, word, image and object . . . [the exhibit] explores the event through the eyes of the participants and examines its impact in 1960. Though centered on the sit-in, the exhibit places the moment within the context of the Civil Rights movement . . . . It tells a limited but complete story . . . . It will continue to remind visitors of the recent nature of the struggle for racial equality and the importance of individual participation in the political process. (Henderson & Kaeppler, 1997, p. 151)

Student curators should think of objects and images as the centerpiece of their display. What objects and images would be most powerful in telling their story? Ask students to make a list of objects and images that are central to their story. Their list may include the following items:

- artifacts (real or created)
- models
- interactive devices
- video presentations
- pictures
- photographs
- graphics
- time lines
- diagrams
- charts
- maps

Students may find the objects and images for their display, ask the community for them, or create them.

Many professional museums begin developing exhibit ideas by looking in their archives for objects and images to help them tell their story. If in-house collections do not provide enough material to carry the story line of their exhibition, museum developers may need to borrow objects from other institutions or people.

For example, the Wisconsin Veterans Museum created an exhibition about intelligence and communication featuring a German Enigma machine, as mentioned in Chapter 5. To create this exhibition, curator of collections William Brewster listened to some of the nearly 500 oral histories archived at the museum. He found excellent stories within these oral histories but needed objects and images to interpret them. Even though the museum's collection was a valuable resource, some

Students at St. Paul's Elementary School built a model of a POW cage and conducted an interview with a former POW as part of their exhibit on Vietnam.

objects had to be acquired from outside sources. For example, the Experimental Aircraft Association Museum in Oshkosh, Wisconsin, provided the museum with cameras, an enlarger, and developing materials, and a private citizen loaned a WWI aerial camera. These objects, along with photographs and interpretive text, completed the exhibition and told the story of intelligence and communication during wartime.

The Seasons of Change Museum at St. Paul's Elementary School is a good example of a project that effectively used objects and images to tell a story. As part of the *Vietnam* exhibit, students created a display about prisoners of war. They felt that a miniature POW cage would draw the attention of visitors and effectively illustrate the conditions that some prisoners endured. Although this type of structure was used only in South Vietnam, Gerald Gerndt, a community member and POW in North Vietnam, experienced similar confinement when he was transported to the prison system for incarceration. Students used their created artifact to discuss Gerndt's POW experience and to explain the differences between Northern and Southern Vietnamese prisons. Further into the exhibit, visitors saw a video interview with Gerndt, conducted by students, and photographs of his return home.

Students from the Alton School District also used a model to tell a story. One of the exhibits for their Black History Museum focused on the sad but important story of Elijah Lovejoy, the editor of the *Alton Observer* in the 1830s. One day as Lovejoy waited for delivery of a printing press, a violent mob opposed to the newspaper's antislavery views

A model depicting events leading up to Elijah Lovejoy's murder was featured in the Alton School District's Black History Museum.

gathered outside the warehouse to protest the delivery. The building was set on fire, Lovejoy was shot and killed, and the press was thrown out the window and destroyed. In their display, students included a model depicting the events leading up to Lovejoy's murder. They also included a reprint of the 1837 newspaper article that described the scene.

In addition to models, students may incorporate other objects into their displays. For a World War II exhibit at Elmwood Elementary School, one student brought in objects her grandfather used during the war—his military jackets, his weekend and holiday pass, a sewing kit—along with some of the medals he was awarded. For an exhibit in their American Revolution Museum, students at Maple Avenue Elementary School created an interactive device—a circuit board question-and-answer game, which was popular with visitors of all ages. To create the game, students built simple circuits inside shirt boxes, using aluminum foil, wire, small light bulbs, and batteries. On the front of each box, students affixed a sheet of paper with a question about their topic and possible matching answers. Visitors used wire probes to select an answer; if they chose correctly, the circuit was completed and lit the bulb.

To incorporate images in their museum, students from Maplewood Richmond Heights Elementary School produced a video presentation for their exhibit about working, living, and playing in their community. In this video, students dressed and played the part of different workers and told viewers about their jobs and contributions to the community. In another creative use of imagery, students from the Alton School District created a mosaic of Martin Luther King Jr. for their Black History Museum.

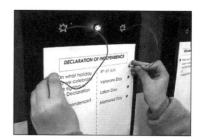

Maple Avenue Elementary School students built a popular circuit board matching game.

Presentation Methods

Museums use a variety of presentation methods to display objects and images. Selecting a presentation method may help students organize the objects and images in their exhibit.

Immersion. The *Streets of Old Milwaukee* at the Milwaukee Public Museum is a life-size re-creation of a 1900s downtown. As visitors stroll down the brick streets, they may peer into the windows of stores, homes, and businesses.

Immersion.

Collection. The Wisconsin Historical Society Museum displays a collection of political campaign buttons of former and current Wisconsin politicians.

Combination. The *Information Age* exhibit at the National Museum of American History shows the history of communication technology using a variety of original source print material, equipment, photographs, and quotations.

Collection.

Demonstration. Many science centers include demonstration exhibits to illustrate a concept or principle. In one such exhibit, visitors look inside a giant kaleidoscope and see reflections of reflections to understand how a handheld kaleidoscope works.

Dramatization. The *A Tribute to Survival* exhibit at the Milwaukee Public Museum features a life-size re-creation of an American Indian powwow.

Combination.

Interactive. Common interactive exhibits include flip-door question-and-answer displays and circuit board matching games. An exhibit at the Saint Louis Zoo's Monsanto Insectarium displays insects, spiders, and millipedes, each with a flip door with the question "Am I an insect?" After examining the live animal in each display case, visitors open the flip door to find the answer and explanation.

Demonstration.

Graphic illustration. In the Saint Louis Zoo's children's area, a life-size cutout includes silhouettes of various animals in the order of their height. Measurements are painted alongside the cutout so children can stand next to it and compare their size to that of each animal.

Testimonial. The *Face to Face: Dealing with Prejudice and Discrimination* exhibit at the Chicago Children's Museum displays video vignettes from various people discussing their experiences with discrimination.

Dramatization.

If students understand exhibit presentation techniques, they can modify them for use in their museum. Students at Elmwood Elementary School developed the design for their

Interactive.

Graphic illustration.

Testimonial.

Great Depression exhibit after they visited *Streets of Old Milwaukee* at the Milwaukee Public Museum. The 6th graders adapted some of the presentation techniques they saw in this immersion gallery. The team created a road leading to a display of photographs from the Great Depression. Along this road, students portrayed desperate Americans in search of work, adding a dramatic element to the exhibit. Tyler, one of the exhibit team members, commented, "The museum put a different perspective on learning. It made me put the work into an exciting presentation to grab the attention of others. I think it was an outstanding way to learn."

The SCAMPER Strategy

SCAMPER is a creative thinking strategy that encourages development of new ideas by rethinking existing ideas (Michalko, 1991, p. 73). By imagining modifications of a product, service, or process that already exists, people create new products, services, and processes. This strategy has been used effectively by businesses.

In the school museum process, the SCAMPER strategy helps trigger students' design ideas. The SCAMPER questions encourage the modification of professional exhibit elements. For example, students at Maple Avenue Elementary School used the SCAMPER strategy to adapt the cutout figures from a professional exhibit for use in their American Revolution Museum. Adding dimension by using cutout figures created visual interest and made their display more engaging than it would have been if it had only included two-dimensional images drawn on posters.

With professional museum exhibits as their inspiration, students modify, adapt, and adjust the designs to create something new for their exhibit. The following SCAMPER questions about professional exhibits will spur creative thought:

• *Substitute:* What can you use instead of the materials, objects, or display methods of this exhibit?

• *Combine:* Which parts or ideas from two different exhibits can you blend together?

• *Adapt:* What part of this exhibit could be copied or imitated, perhaps with a new twist?

• *Modify:* Can you change an attribute of this exhibit such as color, sound, form, or shape?

• *Magnify:* Is there something about this exhibit that could be stronger, larger, higher, exaggerated, or used more frequently?

• *Minimize:* Is there something about this exhibit that could be smaller, lighter, scaled down, or used less frequently?

• *Put to other uses:* Can part of this exhibit be used in a way other than it was intended to be used?

• *Eliminate:* What can you take away or remove from this exhibit?

• *Rearrange:* Can you interchange parts of this exhibit or change its pattern, layout, or sequence?

• *Reverse:* Can you turn parts of this exhibit backward, inside out, upside down, or around?

Students from the Alton School District created a vibrant mosaic of Martin Luther King Jr. for their Black History Museum.

If you choose to visit a professional museum at this point in the process, ask students to use SCAMPER to help them analyze the museum displays. (See Chapter 6 for additional museum visit ideas.)

As students engage in this creative work, some farfetched ideas may emerge. It is important to let them know that "quantity before quality" is one principle of brainstorming. Sometimes crazy ideas lead to new and better suggestions that are later adjusted to become practical (see Michalko, 1991, pp. 295–307). Make sure that your students know the "rules" for brainstorming:

• *Out of the box thinking.* Think of bizarre, off-the-wall, even seemingly impractical ideas. Sometimes the best ideas come from crazy suggestions.

• *No criticism.* All ideas should be accepted. No idea should be seen as too impossible, too inappropriate, or too silly.

- *Quantity.* One of the purposes of brainstorming is to generate a lot of ideas. You will come up with many ideas you cannot use, but in the process you will arrive at several good ideas. In brainstorming, quality comes with quantity.

- *Piggybacking.* Often someone else's idea may trigger an idea by another person in the group. This is called piggybacking. Feel free to modify or expand someone else's idea. Brainstorming is a team activity.

How Will We Get Visitors to Experience Our Story?

The early mission of museums—to discover, collect, classify, and display objects from the natural, geological, and human world—didn't include a strong public education component. Collections of objects were displayed without much thought about learning goals for visitors.

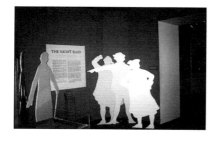

Two-dimensional figures can be staggered to create a three-dimensional display, as shown in this example from the National Museum of American History (top), which inspired students at Maple Avenue Elementary School (bottom).

Now many museum exhibits are interpretive and designed to provide opportunities for visitors to learn. Today's museum professionals design exhibits and labels that "interpret" objects, information, and concepts for the visitor.

The Puelicher Butterfly Wing at the Milwaukee Public Museum has an interpretive gallery outside the glass-enclosed butterfly garden, which houses free-flying butterflies. In this gallery, visitors explore butterfly characteristics, adaptations, life cycles, and diversity. Curator Sue Borkin explains how these interpretive exhibits provide learning opportunities for visitors:

> In addition to the walk-through garden with live butterflies and interpretation provided by docents, we tried to include a variety of age-appropriate and learning style–appropriate opportunities for visitors to examine, experience, and learn about butterflies up close through the use of microscopes, magnifiers, flip panels, enlarged models, photographs, video presentations, computer interactives, costumes, games, and life-size or larger environments.

What principles guide exhibit developers as they improve the interpretative power of their displays? Museum professionals refer to Freeman Tilden as the "father of interpretation." Tilden's (1977) principles of interpretation, written nearly 50 years ago, are still widely used and relevant to museum docents, as well as to label copy writers and exhibit designers:

I. Any interpretation that doesn't somehow relate what is being displayed or described to something within the personality or experience of the visitor will be sterile.

II. Information, as such, is not interpretation. Interpretation is revelation based upon information. But they are entirely different things. However, all interpretation includes information.

III. Interpretation is an art, which combines many arts, whether materials presented are scientific, historical, or architectural. Any art is in some degree teachable.

IV. The chief aim of interpretation is not instruction, but provocation.

V. Interpretation should aim to present a whole rather than a part, and must address the whole man rather than any phase.

VI. Interpretation addressed to children (say, up to the age of 12) should not be a dilution of the presentation to adults, but should follow a fundamentally different approach. To be at its best it will require a separate program. (p. 9)

These principles will be useful as students make decisions about exhibit design. The principles can be simplified for use in school museum projects:

- Relate to the visitor's personal experience.
- Reveal the big idea to the visitor.
- Use creative art forms to help tell the story.
- Encourage the visitor's curiosity, interest, and questions.
- Present a whole story rather than part of a story.

Students who have created school museums understand the importance of reaching their audience, and they are receptive to ideas for improving the interpretive power of their exhibits. As Amanda, a student from Elmwood Elementary school, observed, "Having the audience involved is a good strategy because then it's not so boring. . . . Make your project interesting so that people will want to come and see it."

Relating to the Visitor's Personal Experience

Tilden's first principle of interpretation is reflected in many professional exhibit designs. The Monsanto Insectarium at the Saint Louis Zoo has a cutaway kitchen wall that shows a common insect's habitat—a home. This is a direct attempt to relate the exhibit's message to something the audience knows.

Another Saint Louis Zoo exhibit, *Since You Were Born,* also personalizes its message. Visitors enter their birth date in a touch-screen computer program to see a list of things that have changed since their birth—the number of people born, the number of animals that have become endangered, and the number of homes built.

The Martin Luther King Jr. National Historic Site in Atlanta, Georgia, has an exhibition called *Children of Courage.* One display challenges young people to do what they can to end injustice. A child-size door contains these words: "Who can take the lead in ending injustice? Open the door to see a future leader." The child opens the door and looks into a mirror.

Student curators have also successfully designed displays that relate to the lives of visitors. One effective strategy is to make a comparison between "then" and "now." The History of Our School Museum at St. Paul's Elementary School included an immersion gallery depicting a classroom of the 1950s. In this exhibit, the classroom practices of the 1950s were compared to those of today. Most visitors could relate to the stories, even if they weren't students in the 1950s or 2000s. The

St. Paul's Elementary School students designed a replica of the Vietnam Wall, which listed the names of locals killed in the war, and they encouraged visitors to leave messages.

Seasons of Change Museum at St. Paul's included a replica of the Vietnam Veterans Memorial with the names of local veterans who died in Vietnam. Visitors could write a message and leave it at the Wall, just as people do at the monument in Washington, DC.

Atwater Elementary School students included a "wish tree" in their Japanese Art and Culture exhibition. Visitors were encouraged to write a wish on a piece of paper and hang it on the tree, replicating a custom associated with Tanabata (also known as the star festival in Japan). The wish tree was part of the traveling exhibition that students brought to the Milwaukee Public Museum, and it was such a popular component that students decided to leave it behind for museum visitors. A year later, the tree was still on display in the Asian Exhibit Hall, overflowing with a wide variety of wishes—everything from a wish for world peace to a wish for a new puppy.

Engaging the Visitor's Senses

Displays that engage the senses are more likely to attract and hold the attention of visitors. Students should consider ways to add visual, auditory, kinesthetic, and tactile interest to their exhibits.

For its Seasons of Change Museum about the 1960s, students at St. Paul's Elementary School included a display about the fashions of the era. The backdrop for this exhibit suggested the bold colors and prints that were popular during the decade. Similarly, Elmwood Elementary School students considered the use of color in their exhibit on the Great Depression. As Emily, one of the exhibit designers, explained, "In the Great Depression, people weren't happy, so we're [using] darker colors. We're planning on crumpling the paper [for the label copy] and spilling coffee [on it] and burning the corners so it looks older, as if someone had written it in the 1920s."

Students at St. Paul's Elementary School used bold colors and designs to add visual interest to their 1960s displays.

The use of sound—dramatic readings, music, or special effects—is another way to add interest to a display. Listening to a speech is far more captivating than simply reading it. The students at St. Paul's used sound in their *Civil Rights* exhibit by playing a recording of Martin Luther King Jr.'s "I have a dream" speech (obtained at the local library) in addition to displaying a copy of the text.

Students understand the power of adding an auditory component to their exhibit. In discussing his class's museum project at Elmwood Elementary School, Peter noted that "if you heard music—whether it was creepy, sad, or happy—that music gave you a better feeling for the topic." Megan, another Elmwood student, explained that students "got creative and had movies, quizzes, and music, which really made it sound, not just look, extraordinary."

A noteworthy kinesthetic exhibit is at Carnegie Science Center in Pittsburgh, Pennsylvania. This hands-on science gallery explores the physics of flight, both in the natural and constructed world. One exhibit is about the physics of bird flight. Visitors are asked to walk between two long ribbons of metal with their arms extended. As they do, they trace a figure-eight pattern from one end of the exhibit to the other, simulating the motion of birds' wings in flight.

Similarly, the Field Museum in Chicago has an exhibit called *Underground Adventure*. Visitors enter this gallery by traveling down a

The *Wright Brothers* exhibit at Randall Elementary School's innovation museum featured a listening station.

"tunnel" that shrinks them to 1/100 of their normal size. (The illusion of shrinking is created by gradually changing the size of objects on the walls of the tunnel.) Once in the gallery, visitors are "underground" and able to see the tremendous variety of plant and animal life that lives in the soil just a few inches below the surface.

Students in kindergarten through 2nd grade at St. Paul's Elementary School created a museum called Neighborhoods Near and Far. An exhibit on Thailand used many exhibit techniques common in children's museums and offered numerous kinesthetic and tactile experiences for visitors. Young visitors had an opportunity for hands-on experiences including writing in Thai, using chopsticks, tasting typical Thai foods, riding a *tuk-tuk* (a three-wheel mode of public transportation), sitting on a life-size cardboard cutout of an elephant (the national animal of Thailand), and purchasing produce in an outdoor Thai market.

Another example of incorporating a hands-on approach comes from the American Revolution Museum at Maple Avenue Elementary School. A kiosk featured life-size paintings of King George and three colonists, one painting on each side of the kiosk. Text was suspended inside the kiosk, and visitors could peer through peephole eyes to read differing perspectives of the British involvement in the colonies. This simple enhancement of the display made it quite popular among visitors.

What Will Our Completed Exhibit Look Like?

Most students and teachers have never designed three-dimensional, museum-style displays. Some are intimidated by this challenge and feel uncertain about their ability to generate visually appealing display ideas that are affordable and appropriate for the exhibit. Even these students and teachers find interesting design solutions for their exhibits and are able to successfully plan their exhibition space.

A kinesthetic exhibit at the Carnegie Science Center enables visitors to experience the physics involved in flight.

The Thai market at the Neighborhoods Near and Far Museum at St. Paul's Elementary School provided a hands-on experience for visitors.

Using Inexpensive Materials

Creative displays can be made from ordinary supplies such as heavy cardboard, old shipping boxes, butcher paper, tension string, and paint. With a little scavenging, interesting solutions can be found; donations of "junk" from home add even more options. Examples of interesting display ideas using inexpensive, easily accessible materials follow.

• The kiosks in the Maple Avenue American Revolution museum were made using $4' \times 8'$ Styrofoam insulation boards available from most home improvement stores. The boards were connected to one another with long screws.

• A kiosk used in St. Paul's Seasons of Change Museum was created by staggering painted boxes on top of one other to display political cartoons of the 1960s.

• Rather than affix a large cardboard panel to the wall, a St. Paul's teacher volunteered to make simple stands from scrap wood. This creative solution ensured that the panels about the 1960s were portable and not restricted by available wall space.

• At Atwater Elementary School, students made an Aztec temple and mural from sheets of large cardboard and Sculptamold, a commercial molding product. In art class, students made Aztec symbols from clay, placed them on Styrofoam meat trays, and covered them with Sculptamold. Once dry, the mold was removed, leaving brick forms that were later painted, glued onto a large piece of cardboard, and propped up on a stand for the Fiesta del Arte Museum.

• Panels of butcher paper suspended from the ceiling created the illusion of a room in an Elmwood Elementary School exhibit about the history of the Olympics.

• Students from the Alton School District created a large box of crayons to accompany a poem about diversity for one of their Black History Museum exhibits. The crayons were made with brightly colored sheets of butcher paper rolled into cylinders.

Planning the Exhibition Space

Depending on where your museum will be housed, you may need a scale drawing for the entire exhibition floor plan. For example, the American Revolution Museum at Maple Avenue Elementary School was housed in a multipurpose room for three weeks of the school year. This large, rectangular room comfortably held seven exhibits. Before students developed their individual displays, they needed to know how much space they could use.

Developing a floor plan for the exhibition may involve the entire class, or the task could be assigned to a smaller group. Either way, the floor plan should specify the amount of space allotted for each display and the anticipated path of the visitor. Consideration must be given to traffic flow through the exhibition, even though most visitors don't follow prescribed paths. Figure 8.2 on p. 132 shows a sample floor plan for a nine-exhibit museum. This very simple plan is useful as an example, but students may wish to be more creative in their designs.

Visitors to the American Revolution Museum at Maple Avenue Elementary School looked through peepholes to read exhibit text.

Once there is an overall floor plan for the exhibition, exhibit groups plan for their allotted space. Students may use graph paper to map out their display, using a scale that roughly corresponds to the square footage of their exhibit area. Alternatively, students may create a small three-dimensional mock-up of their display. Many school museum exhibits use display boards—an existing wall, a portable bulletin board, or a panel that has been constructed from cardboard, foam core, grid wire, screening, or some other material. Students plan this space as well. Students old enough to create their own drawings should do so; if they are too young, teachers, older students, or other adults can assist. The exhibition floor plan and drawings or mock-ups of exhibit displays will become the blueprints for construction.

Will Our Exhibit Work?

Museum professionals conduct three forms of exhibit evaluation: (1) front-end evaluation, when they find out what visitors know, feel, and think about the topic and incorporate these perceptions into the design of the exhibit (see Chapter 5); (2) formative evaluation, when they present drawings or mock-ups to visitors to see how they respond to the material; and (3) summative evaluation, when they evaluate visitor responses to the exhibition in terms of its appeal and its effect on learning, feeling, and action (see Chapter 12).

After students have designed their exhibits, they can conduct formative evaluation to improve their designs. Though museum professionals typically conduct formative evaluation with a prototype exhibit complete with copy, students can conduct a simplified version using their drawings. They can ask students from other exhibit teams, other students in the school, parents, or other adults to respond to their exhibit ideas. The following evaluation questions developed by Serrell (1996, p. 141) might be useful during the formative evaluation process:

- Do they like it?
- Do they think it is fun?
- Do they understand it?
- Do they find it meaningful?
- Does their understanding coincide with (or at least not contradict) the stated communication objectives for the element?
- Does it give the user a sense of discovery, wonder, or "wow"?

Based on what students learn from the formative evaluation, they may want to brainstorm alternative, better ways to design their exhibits.

Summary

Designing the school exhibition occurs after research is complete and students have an adequate answer to their focus question. They begin to imagine how they will interpret the message of their exhibit using objects, images, and experiences—tools to help tell the

Students can create appealing displays for their school museums using accessible and inexpensive materials.

Figure 8.2
Floor Plan

This 49′ × 30′ space will house a nine-exhibit museum. Each exhibit has a maximum of 120 square feet (8′ × 15′) of space. Aisles have been included in the floor plan.

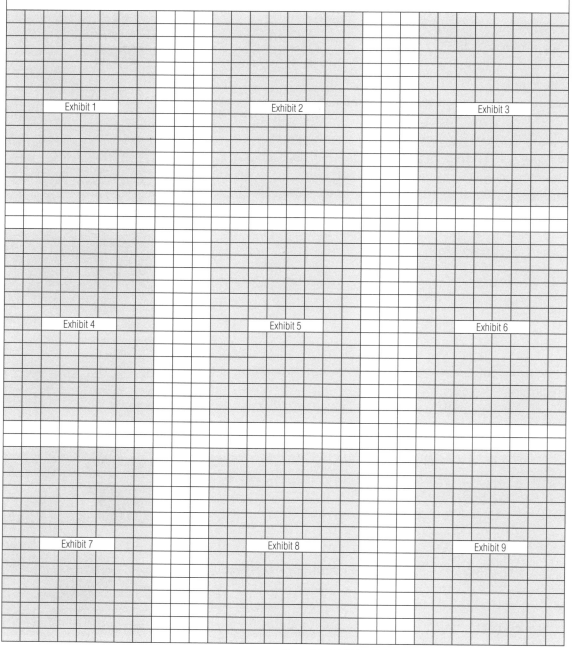

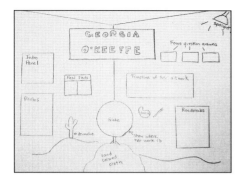 

A detailed drawing of a display, prepared during the design phase, becomes a useful guide later for the actual construction of the exhibit.

story. Reviewing various presentation methods and professional exhibits helps students design displays that visitors will relate to and find appealing. Once students have decided what their displays will look like, they can ask potential visitors for input before beginning the next step of the school museum process—writing label copy.

9

Writing for a Museum Audience

Seventh graders Emily, Danny, Zack, and Anita gather around a table to examine their exhibit drawing and review the objects that they selected to tell their exhibit story. They are now ready to interpret these objects and images with text. The students assign the writing tasks among themselves; they will work independently for several days. As Danny gets ready to write his text panel—label copy for a cluster of objects grouped together by theme—he reviews the team's visitor learning goals and research findings. He makes a list of the important points he will highlight in his writing and thinks about ways to relate these points to visitors' experiences. After he completes his first draft, he uses a rubric to evaluate and revise his work. The next day he shares his writing with a peer editor and brainstorms presentation techniques that will make the text more readable and appealing. Later that week, when team members have finished their assignments, they meet to assess their collective writing, which results in some minor adjustments for each student. The students review their exhibit design and decide to add an introductory panel, captions for their objects and images, directions for their interactive devices, and a title that clearly communicates the big idea of their exhibit.

Students have completed research for their focus questions; selected images, artifacts, and objects for their exhibit; and developed a drawing or mock-up of their display. They may have tested their concept on potential audiences and made adjustments based on feedback (formative evaluation). They are now ready to write text for their exhibit. Museum professionals refer to the text as *label copy*, which includes exhibit titles, captions, and interpretive text panels.

Ideally, writing will precede construction. Writing is difficult work, typically less exciting for students than construction. Once construction begins, students are very enthusiastic, and momentum builds as the opening event approaches. To pause after construction and ask students to write copy for their exhibit is somewhat anticlimactic and likely to result in a less thoughtful product. Have students write first; the promise of construction will sustain them.

Label copy interprets an exhibit's objects, images, and experiences. To write effective copy, students must consider their audience—museum visitors don't spend much time reading. Students must write succinctly, developing the most important, engaging, and powerful points from their research notes. To do this they must analyze, synthesize, and paraphrase research information and connect it to exhibit content. These essential skills aren't taught in isolation, but anchored in the purposeful work of exhibit development.

Students at Elmwood Elementary School develop their writing skills as they work on their school museum project.

This authentic writing task forces students to clarify their purpose for writing and to write appropriately for their audience. In this project, students write for a challenging audience—people of all ages, abilities, and interests who are reading in an environment that is busy and active. This challenge is likely to sharpen student awareness of purpose and audience and to improve their writing overall.

In *Exhibit Labels: An Interpretive Approach* (1996), Serrell lists 10 "deadly sins" of label copy:

  1. Labels that are not related to a big idea, that ramble without focus or objectives.
  2. Labels that have too much emphasis on instruction (presenting information) instead of interpretation (offering provocation).
  3. Labels that do not address visitors' prior knowledge, interests, and/or misconceptions—that don't know who the audience is.
  4. Labels with no apparent system of design and content to organize the messages, codes, or context.

    5. Labels written with vocabulary that is out of reach for the majority of visitors.

    6. Labels that are too long and wordy.

    7. Labels that ask questions that are not visitors' questions.

    8. Labels for interactives that do not have instructions or interpretations located in integrated, logical ways.

    9. Labels that do not begin with concrete, visual references.

    10. Labels that are hard to read because of poor typography (bad choice of typeface, design, colors, lighting, materials, or placement). (pp. 233–234)

You and your students will recognize many of these deadly sins in museum exhibits you have visited. You may find it useful to review this list with your students before beginning the writing process.

Five Traits of Label Copy

For most students, museum visitors will be the most unique audience for whom they have written. Students will need support as they translate their research notes into effective museum copy. As they write, students should be aware of the key traits of label copy: content and organization, relevance, voice, presentation, and grammar.

Photographs of text from professional museum exhibits (or samples of anonymous class work) can provide useful models of strong and weak label copy. Students can analyze these samples and use a rubric to assess them (see Figure 9.1 on pp. 138–139). This exercise will deepen students' understanding of the rubric and help them monitor their own work in progress. They should also use the rubric to regularly evaluate their label copy.

Content and Organization

The content and organization of exhibit text should help visitors understand the big idea and key points of the display. Label copy should focus on the visual material of the exhibit. Remind students that they were asked to tell their exhibit story without words when they selected objects and images during the design phase of the project. Now, as they write copy, they should connect new information to what the visitor can see in their display.

In addition, the content should be original. Emphasize that students must write text in their own words and not copy from their source material, unless they are including a direct quotation.

Students know the big idea of their exhibit and the various images, objects, and experiences included in their display. They use this information to create a text plan for their exhibit—a list of the interpretive labels, captions, and noninterpretive labels (credit panels, orientation signs, and so on) that they will write. They also develop a title for their exhibit; this may be the focus question or a statement that communicates the big idea of their display. Completing a planning form, such as the one shown in Figure 9.2 on p. 140, is a good way for student teams to get organized. Teams use the form to determine what label copy their exhibit needs and who will write it.

Relevance

As discussed in Chapter 8, displays should be relevant to visitors. It is also important that label copy be relevant. Text is useful to the visitor when it provides something to "do" intellectually: agree or disagree with an idea, make a decision, draw a conclusion, or discover something new (Serrell, 1996, p. 83). Text may also encourage dialogue among groups of visitors—an excellent indicator that it is meaningful. The following techniques may help your students make exhibit text relevant for visitors:

• Ask a question to engage the visitor. This may be a question the visitor might have, or it may be a thought-provoking question that you create.

• Write about an experience or feeling common to most people.

• Include a suitable quotation that draws visitors into the content of your exhibit.

• Encourage participation among visitors. This can be done by raising questions, presenting ideas, or suggesting an activity.

The Martin Luther King Jr. National Historic Site in Atlanta, Georgia, makes effective use of provocative questions in its *Children of Courage* exhibition. Visitors see a large photo of King and the quotation "Life's most persistent and urgent question is, 'What are you doing for others?'" The exhibition features displays that pose a series of questions about injustice in the world and encourage visitors to take action.

Anticipating visitors' questions is another strategy that makes exhibit text relevant. The *Children of Courage* exhibition includes a flip-door display that presents a protest photograph from the civil rights movement and asks visitors "Why is this black student braving an angry crowd?" Visitors open the flip door to find the answer: "To integrate a public school."

Figure 9.1
Rubric for Label Copy

Trait	Excellent 5	Very Good 4	Adequate 3	Needs Improvement 2	Not Acceptable 1
Content and organization: **The content and order of our exhibit labels help visitors understand our big idea.**					
Our exhibit title communicates the big idea of our exhibit and captures visitors' attention.					
Our interpretive text panels are written in short paragraphs that address one key idea at a time and are accompanied by a visual device.					
Our captions clearly label specific objects, artifacts, images, and interactive devices.					
We include noninterpretive labels when appropriate (credit panels, orientation signs, etc.).					
Relevance: **Our writing is relevant and useful to the visitor.**					
Our text is relevant to visitors because it relates to their personal experience, asks a question they might ask, poses a provocative question, or includes a quotation that draws them into the content.					
Our text is useful to visitors because it gives them something to "do" intellectually (agree or disagree with an idea, make a decision, draw a conclusion, or discover something new).					
Our text encourages conversation among visitors.					
Voice: **The tone of our writing is clear and consistent.**					
Our copy is written in a consistent voice, and it is clear who is "speaking" to the visitor (the school, an expert, a friend, a specific real or fictitious personality, etc.).					
The voice of the writer conveys enthusiasm for the topic.					
Our language is clear; technical terms are used when appropriate and explained to the visitor.					

Figure 9.1 *(continued)*
Rubric for Label Copy

Trait	Excellent 5	Very Good 4	Adequate 3	Needs Improvement 2	Not Acceptable 1
Presentation: **The visual quality, organization, and structure of our text make it easy to read.**					
We use typographic devices to make key points obvious (e.g., bullet points to highlight certain ideas; italics, underlining, and boldface to make words stand out; and variations in font and size for emphasis).					
Our text is visible to the visitor; we use 20-point font or greater for body text and 28-point to 48-point font for titles or text to be read at a distance, and we place copy within the visitor's field of vision.					
Our text panels are appropriate for a museum audience—50 words or fewer per panel.					
Our text is legible, presented in a readable font and with high-contrast typography.					
Grammar: **The text in our exhibit is grammatically correct.**					
Our text panels are grammatically correct, are free of spelling errors, and include proper punctuation.					

Label copy score: _____

How could you improve? List one or two goals for upcoming work.

_____

_____

_____

_____

Figure 9.2
Exhibit Text Planning Worksheet

Step 1: List your focus question and develop an exhibit title. Your exhibit title may be the same as your focus question, or it could be a statement that communicates the big idea of your exhibit, captures visitors' attention, or hints at content to come.

Step 2: Look at your exhibit drawing and make a list of all the interpretive labels that you will need. These panels relate the key points of your exhibit to the visual devices in your display. They may also pose provocative questions, feature suitable quotations, or anticipate visitors' questions.

Step 3: Decide who will write each interpretive label. Make sure each student on your team writes at least one.

Step 4: Make a list of all the captions that you will need. Captions identify your exhibit's objects, images, artifacts, interactive devices, or other display items.

Step 5: Make a list of all the noninterpretive labels (if any) that you will need. Noninterpretive labels include credit panels, orientation signs, and the like.

Step 6: Decide who will write each caption and noninterpretive label.

Focus Question:

Exhibit Title:

Interpretive Label	Student
Caption	**Student**
Noninterpretive Label	**Student**

Quotations can be effective at drawing visitors into an exhibit. The Museum of Westward Expansion in St. Louis, Missouri, uses quotations exclusively—the "story" is told through first-person quotations from people represented in the exhibits. Although this approach may not be suitable for your school museum, the use of carefully selected quotations can add interest to your displays and bring emotional relevance to your exhibition.

Voice

Making label copy relevant to visitors will encourage them to read it. But interest will wane unless copy is written in language understandable to the audience and presented with a clear and consistent "voice." The voice of the exhibit might be that of an expert, a friend, or a specific personality (real or fictitious), or it might be the combination of more than one voice (Serrell, 1996). As students write exhibit text, they should consider the following questions:

- Who is speaking to the visitor in the exhibit?
- Does the copy convey enthusiasm for the topic?
- Does the copy grab and hold the visitor's attention?

Because individual students write copy for the exhibit, it is important for teams to edit collective work for one consistent voice.

Presentation

Relevant copy will attract visitors. Text with a strong voice will hold visitors. And good presentation of copy will encourage visitors to read everything. When exhibit text is presented well, it is of an appropriate length, includes helpful typographic devices, and is clearly visible.

Length. Visitors will not read long paragraphs of text in a museum. Therefore, students will have to write copy that is crisp, clear, and to the point. Students will learn a great deal about their topic as they conduct research, and they may not be able to write about everything. They will need to make their points powerfully and succinctly.

Maplewood Richmond Heights Elementary School students wrote brief captions for the objects in their displays.

According to Serrell (1996), if labels contain 50 or fewer words, more visitors will read them and read them more completely. Students may create several sections of text per exhibit; but even with multiple panels, drafting concise and powerful statements will be your students' most demanding writing challenge. (This paragraph contains 53 words!)

To emphasize the importance of writing copy that is of an appropriate length for a museum audience, ask students to recall the text panels they saw at the professional museum they visited. How much time did they spend reading? Why wouldn't they want to stand for long periods of time to read text? Their answers may include the following observations:

- There are many exhibits to see in the museum, and they don't want to spend too much time at a few and miss the rest.
- They are more interested in the objects in the exhibit, so they read the headings and main points quickly.
- It is hard to concentrate on long text panels because there are a lot of people in the museum and a lot of activity and noise.
- After about an hour or so, they begin to get tired and have a hard time taking in more information.

Students at Maplewood Richmond Heights Elementary School prepare text for their exhibit.

Discussing the way students reacted to exhibit text as visitors will help them write their own exhibit text.

Students might have difficulty with the 50-word limit. Ask your students what problems this limitation might place on them as authors. They might express some of these common responses:

- We have a lot of information in our notes that will be hard to condense.
- We may not be able to use all of our information.
- It will be hard to decide what to include and what to leave out.
- The copy may not make sense if it is too choppy.

As students consider such challenges, encourage them to review the big idea of the exhibition and the story line of their exhibit, which should help them focus on what material to select.

Typographic devices. Typography can enhance key ideas in student text panels, especially when copy is succinct. Bullet points can make text easier to read; italics, underlining, and boldface can make important words stand out; and font sizes and styles can add emphasis. Presentation devices help students emphasize the significant points of their exhibit. Lauren, a 6th grader at Elmwood Elementary School, explains how her World War II exhibit team approached their label copy:

There are a bunch of battles that go on during the war and certain ones are [more] important, [like the] Battle of the Bulge. . . . [We used] fancy scissors to make it stand out because it was one of the last battles, and it has to do with our interview. . . . The things that stand out the most are what we want [the visitor] to know.

Visibility. Sometimes students write label copy that is well organized and relevant to visitors and that has a strong, consistent, and appropriate voice . . . and visitors still walk by. Why? The text may be difficult to read, perhaps because it is too small or placed on a background color that doesn't provide adequate contrast. Students should pay attention to the traits in the label copy rubric and be certain that their text is visible and easy to read. For professional museums, Serrell (1996) recommends nothing less than 20-point font for body text and 28-point to 48-point font for titles or text to be read at a distance.

Grammar

Last but not least, students need to edit their copy for grammar, spelling, and punctuation. Like any text prepared for readers, label copy should be free of errors. Students' finished written products should reflect the effort and care they put into the entire exhibit development process. Grammatical errors distract visitors and can signal sloppy work, creating a bad impression that could be generalized to research, design, and writing efforts. Encourage students to use peer, adult, or teacher editors to review their draft work and make sure it is grammatically correct.

Guided Practice

Once students have had a chance to consider the traits of high-quality writing, consider modeling the writing process for them using research notes. If you used the guided research lesson in Chapter 7, students will have notes from research they read (pertinent to your exhibition theme). Select one student's notes and use them to write an introductory panel for the museum.

Students can practice writing by using research notes from one exhibit group. Small teams of students can review the key research findings from this volunteer group and use them to write label copy. The full class can then evaluate small-group writing samples using the label copy rubric.

Independent Writing

Using their research notes, students write label copy independently. You may want to give them a worksheet for their first draft (see Figure 9.3). During independent writing time, students should ask peers to edit their work as it is developing, using the label copy rubric to offer feedback. Structured peer-editing sessions work well, and the three-minute conference strategy (see Figure 4.4 on p. 56) may provide a useful format for peer feedback.

Students at Elmwood Elementary School review their team's research findings in preparation for writing label copy.

If students are having difficulty with independent writing, consider presenting a mini-lesson on a particular trait from the rubric. For example, you may select a piece of your own writing that illustrates the common problem and then let students analyze it and make suggestions for improvement. They can also use anonymous class work to brainstorm advice for the author, focusing improvement suggestions on a single trait. Then students can use that advice to revise their own work.

As students engage in independent writing, they use the label copy rubric to assess their work. And as students review several drafts of their work, they can reflect on their progress over time. To assess their progress, students might use a reflective writing prompt such as "I am becoming a better writer. I used to . . . , and now I . . ." or "Here is what I've learned . . . Here is what I need to work on . . ."

Labels for the Full Exhibition

After exhibit labels are written and team members share them with one another, the full class can develop label copy for the museum as a whole. Serrell (1996) notes that exhibitions typically include the following label copy:

- an exhibition title that arouses the visitor's interest and curiosity
- an introductory panel that introduces the big idea of the museum and provides the visitor with an orientation to the space

Figure 9.3
Label Copy Worksheet

Step 1: Review the text plan for your exhibit.

Step 2: As a team, write a title for each text panel. This header could be the focus question, a variation of the focus question, or a phrase that captures the main point of the exhibit component. Use a separate worksheet for each header.

Step 3: Draft the label copy for which you are responsible.

Step 4: Share your draft with teammates and make adjustments based on their feedback.

Exhibit: _____   **Component:** _____

Header:

Label Copy:

• a concluding label that provides closure, reinforcement, or new insight for the visitor

Once students have a final draft of the label copy for their exhibits and the exhibition as a whole, they may type it up or you may consider asking parent volunteers to do this. You can enlarge text using a poster maker or software programs that create large text panels. With their final text in hand, students are ready to begin construction.

Summary

Exhibit titles, captions, and text panels interpret the exhibit's objects, images, and experiences. Museum professionals refer to the text in these panels as label copy. Student curators develop a text plan for their exhibit that lists all the label copy they will write.

The traits of writing in a school museum project include content and organization, relevance, voice, presentation, and grammar. Writing label copy for the school museum is an opportunity for your students to develop their skill in writing for a particular purpose and specific audience.

Writing instruction includes modeling, guided practice, and independent writing with plenty of feedback—from teachers, peers, and other adults. Students may need mini-lessons focused on one or more rubric traits if they run into difficulty writing.

As a group, students may want to write copy for the full exhibition. This copy might include an exhibition title, introductory panel, and concluding label.

10

Constructing the Exhibition

Eighth graders Maxine, Sarah, Drew, and Ian are sitting in a circle on the floor, updating their construction plan. They made excellent progress yesterday and are pleased to remove several items from their to-do list. They review their updated plan and decide what to accomplish today: Drew and Maxine will continue building the three-dimensional model they started yesterday, and Ian and Sarah will paint display panels so that they can affix label copy and images to them tomorrow.

Five other groups are also busy at work. One exhibit team is affixing text panels to their display. Another is assembling interactive circuit boards. A different team is in the computer lab, editing their video presentation. Everywhere you look, clusters of students are working on different tasks, using different materials, and solving different problems; and all are surprisingly self-directed. These 8th grade students are working productively in an environment that, at least for a few days, feels less like a school and more like a design studio.

After completing the hard work of research, exhibit design, and writing, students are eager to construct their displays. This part of the project is most unlike typical school, and it offers unique opportunities for students who have strengths and talents beyond academics. A teacher from St. Paul's Elementary School observed the change in her class during the construction phase: "I was amazed at how excited some of the kids got about the project. I [saw] strengths [in] students I normally would not have seen [in] regular classroom instruction."

Creating a school museum engages students in a variety of instructional activities that suit the multiple intelligences proposed by Howard Gardner (1983, 1993). Gardner suggests that although schools traditionally favor logical/mathematical intelligence, there are many ways in which people are "smart." A museum project permits students to express their understanding through visual/spatial, musical, verbal, interpersonal, intrapersonal, and bodily/kinesthetic intelligences.

Students at Maplewood Richmond Heights Elementary School assemble materials for their museum displays.

The power of a classroom culture that encourages intelligence to be expressed in a variety of ways is illustrated by the story of "Jason," a student involved in a social studies exhibition. Not viewed as a strong academic student, Jason was typically ignored by his peers. While researching and writing for his team's exhibit, Jason did struggle. But when it came time to plan the museum installation, Jason's visual/spatial abilities were an enormous asset. He was able to visualize three-dimensional exhibits and represent them in two-dimensional diagrams. Classmates asked Jason for his assistance with mechanical issues that emerged unexpectedly. This opportunity to excel gave Jason new status and redefined for his classmates what it meant to be smart. He was viewed in a new light and was respected as a skilled and intelligent colleague by his peers.

Construction and installation is not "time off" from school; it is a time for all students to deepen their teamwork skills, learn organization skills, develop artistic sensibility, and improve visual and spatial awareness. It is also fun for students; most will say it is the best part of the project. This incentive is useful—it spurs on the hard work of research, writing, and design that precedes construction. And the completed museum itself provides incentive for yet more learning, when students teach visitors what they know.

View the construction phase as an important time filled with learning. When you hold your students to the same disciplined planning required in all previous steps, construction and installation will be every bit as smooth and productive.

Organizing for Construction

Before students dive headlong into construction, have them create a plan for their upcoming work. This plan is a valuable tool when enthusi-asm is high and ideas abound. Teachers know that positive student energy can quickly regress into chaos if it is not directed. But part of the discipline of school museum work is planning before moving ahead, and students should be accustomed to it by this point in the project.

Students should complete a formal construction plan (see Figure 10.1 on p. 150). The plan will outline tasks that the team must accomplish in the upcom-ing days, who will complete them, and when they should be done. At the end of each day, the team uses the plan to

St. Paul's Elementary School students begin the construction phase of their Neighborhoods Near and Far Museum.

review its progress and make adjustments as needed. Although detailed planning does take time, it will definitely save time in the long run.

Additionally, students should list all the materials, supplies, and equipment necessary to construct their exhibit. This way, they can assemble everything they need before they begin construction. If a material, supply, or piece of equipment is not available, students will have time to make adjustments to the exhibit design. They can use a worksheet, such as the one shown in Figure 10.2 on p. 151, to keep track of construction materials. (Alternatively, this can be done during the design phase, when students create their drawings.)

Randall Elementary School students work in teams to construct and install the displays for their innovation museum.

Figure 10.1
Construction Planning Worksheet

Step 1: List all tasks that need to be accomplished.

Step 2: As a team, divide the tasks among yourselves.

Step 3: Create a time line for accomplishing the tasks and checking in with the team.

Step 4: Meet regularly to update your plan and make adjustments as needed.

Exhibit: _____

Task	Student	Due Date

Working as a Team

Teamwork is important throughout the school museum project and especially during construction. If needed, ask students to engage in a collaborative, easy first task before they move on to the more complicated and less predictable work of construction. For example, mounting label copy on colored paper before affixing it to the display is an easy team task and gives the display a more finished look. After teams have completed this task, they can self-assess their teamwork skills using a rubric for teamwork (see Figure 5.5 on p. 78). If certain skills need further practice, you may wish to prepare a mini-lesson on teamwork, such as the one described in Chapter 5.

Installing the Museum

When students have completed construction of their displays, they are ready to install the exhibits in the museum space. This is a good time to invite community participation—parents, community members, even

---

Figure 10.2
Materials, Supplies, and Equipment Worksheet

Step 1: Review your exhibit drawing and make a list of the artifacts, images, and objects in your display. Also list all the other materials that you will need to create your display, such as batteries, hinges, buzzers, and shirt boxes.

Step 2: Make a list of all the supplies that you will need to create your exhibit, such as card stock, butcher paper, double-sided tape, adhesive spray, scissors, and rulers.

Step 3: Make a list of all the equipment that you will need to create your exhibit, such as a slide projector, a TV/DVD player, a tape recorder, light sources, and extension cords.

Exhibit: _____

Materials	Supplies	Equipment

---

other teachers may be happy to help install student exhibits. Consider recruiting volunteers for a special "installation day" to set up the museum. (See Chapter 2 for more on involving the community in the museum installation process.)

Summary

Students enjoy the construction and installation phase of the school museum project, which allows them to develop and use visual, spatial, kinesthetic, and mechanical skills not typically required in school. It is a time when problem-solving, teamwork, and organizational skills are developed and honed.

The construction process provides incentive for previous work and creates context for upcoming learning (when students explain their exhibits to the visiting public). To make it a productive time, students should develop a construction plan and a list of the materials, supplies, and equipment they will need to create their display. Finally, student teams must meet regularly to update their plan. With careful preparation on the part of students, there is no reason why the construction and installation phase of the school museum project can't be both fun and productive.

11

Learning the Full Exhibition

The 4th grade class is seated on the floor, facing the exhibit developed by Benjamin, Allison, Morgan, and Terrance. These four students give a brief presentation about their exhibit while classmates—with pens and worksheets in hand—listen attentively, taking notes. Up to this point, each 4th grader worked on one exhibit; now students will learn the content of the full museum. They want to speak knowledgably about the full exhibition on opening night, but they are listening attentively for another reason as well—they will be assessed on their understanding of the entire museum.

Allison gives an overview of her team's exhibit, including the focus question and the key points covered in her team's display. Terrance presents the first point, using objects and artifacts to explain important facts, examples, and details. Morgan and Benjamin do the same for the remaining portions of the exhibit. The team members answer several of their classmates' questions before it is time for the next exhibit team to give its presentation.

Your completed school museum is a wonderful learning resource. Honor the hard work of your students by teaching from their exhibits, and encourage them to teach one another about their displays. If possible, install the museum at least a week before the opening so that students will have time to learn the entire exhibition.

Asking students to lead exhibition tours provides leverage for learning. If students are required to play the role of knowledgeable staff during the public opening, they will be motivated to learn the content in the full exhibition. In addition, remind students that to achieve their knowledge learning target, they must be able to answer each of the focus questions in the school museum.

Consider using the completed displays to deliver a series of guided lessons. This is motivating to students—it is unusual for their work to become the "text" for classroom activities. You might base a lesson on Merrill Harmin's (1994) "speak-write" strategy, which consists of a short lecture with regular pauses for students to write personal reactions, summaries, or questions (p. 38). You might organize your lecture around several key points related to a focus question. Using this strategy, the lecture would last several minutes, followed by a brief pause when students write. You would then resume speaking for several minutes, followed by another pause, and so on. Harmin suggests "augmenting lectures with lots of visuals" (p. 39)—this is an easy task with the exhibit close at hand! After the lecture, students might pair up to compare notes and discuss questions. Younger students can write, draw, or just think before sharing their summary, question, or reaction with a partner. This sharing might be followed by a large-group discussion.

Preparing for Interpretation

Those who interact with museum visitors are called docents or interpreters. Your students will play this role on opening night. They will draw visitors to their display, show or explain something about the exhibit, pose questions, or answer questions.

To prepare students for their role, you may want to discuss the modified version of Tilden's principles of interpretation listed on p. 125 of Chapter 8. The principles of interpretation help students consider ways to effectively interact with visitors. Students who have developed strategies for engaging their visitors feel more effective as docents. Derek, a student from Elmwood Elementary School, explains that being a docent "made me feel proud of myself because I was teaching people many things and passing on information that I hoped they would find interesting."

Jim Jordan, associate curator of education at the Saint Louis Zoo, uses Tilden's principles when training zoo interpreters. He wants interpreters to capture visitors' interest by holding demonstrations and simulations, portraying characters, and interacting with artifacts and exhibits. The intention of these activities is to provoke visitors' questions or to present ideas and issues that visitors may not come to on their own.

Jordan shared the docent interpretation worksheet that he uses at the zoo with teachers at Maplewood Richmond Heights Elementary School as they designed a rainforest exhibit (see Figure 11.1 on p. 156). The worksheet is used to develop a "hook" to engage visitors—in this case, it was used to plan an activity about animal adaptations. You may want to use this worksheet with your class to collaboratively plan interpretation activities for one or more of your exhibits.

To develop hooks that capture the attention of museum visitors, students will use the big idea and story line of their exhibit to generate ideas. These hooks can be questions, objects, pictures, or activities that will engage visitors and help interpret the exhibit. For example, for their exhibit about the Wright brothers, student interpreters at Randall Elementary School asked visitors to think about how their lives would be different if there were no air travel. The question prompted lively discussion, which gave students the opportunity to explain some of the key points in their display.

Teaching One Another

Students use their displays to teach one another the content in their exhibit. Because every student will act as a museum staff member during the opening, students have a real reason to listen as peers review exhibit content. Rehearsing for opening night will prepare students for the event. The strategies that follow can help students deepen their knowledge as they prepare.

Team Presentations

Each exhibit team may give a brief presentation to the rest of the class. Presentations might last about five minutes and include the following:

- the exhibit focus question
- answers to the focus question in the form of key points (these will be similar to the story line statements or visitor learning goals that exhibit teams developed)

Students at Randall Elementary School teach one another about their displays.

Figure 11.1
Docent Interpretation Worksheet

Topic:
Animal adaptations

Hook (a question, object, picture, or activity that captures the visitor's attention):
Try to unbutton your shirt without using your thumb. Can you do it?

Idea 1:
Opposable thumbs are adaptations that help primates live in a forest habitat.

Supporting Fact 1:
Primates have the ability to grasp tree limbs and climb trees.

Supporting Fact 2:
Monkeys and apes also have opposable big toes that allow them to grasp objects with both their hands and feet.

Idea 2:
Some monkeys, like spider monkeys from Central America, have a prehensile tail—a "fifth hand."

Supporting Fact 1:
Spider monkeys can use their tail to grasp branches and hang from trees.

Supporting Fact 2:
Spider monkeys are built for living in trees and are very adept at traveling through treetops.

Conclusion (memorable thought or message that ties everything together or that provides information for action):
Each animal has physical traits that help it survive in the habitat it lives in. People have opposable thumbs. How do we use this adaptation?

• support for each key point—details, facts, and examples
• the exhibit's artifacts, objects, and images and their relationship to the focus question
• ideas for interacting with visitors

A short question-and-answer session might follow each presentation.

As students listen to class presentations, they take notes to help them learn the content of each exhibit and understand the museum project as a whole. A sample note-taking form is presented in Figure 11.2.

Figure 11.2
Exhibit Presentation Worksheet

Step 1: List the exhibit title and its focus question.

Step 2: Listen carefully to your classmates as they explain their exhibit and answer their focus question.

Step 3: List the key points of the exhibit and any important supporting information—details, facts, and examples.

Step 4: Explain how the artifacts, objects, and images support the key point.

Exhibit:

Focus Question:

Key Points:

Supporting details, facts, and examples:

Supporting artifacts, objects, and images:

Concept Maps

If students created a concept map for the school museum at the introduction of the project, they may update their map as a way to learn the full exhibition (see Figure 5.3 on p. 69). Students who did not create a concept map at the outset may create one at this point in the project using their overview notes from class presentations.

Students can use the concept map of the full exhibition to organize their knowledge of the museum topic, as the map now includes answers to each focus question. Encourage students to make connections among and between focus questions and key points to help them see how the various exhibits fit into the whole exhibition.

Tour Scripts

Students may use their overview notes and concept map to create a short tour script for the entire museum. Most visitors want some free time to explore the museum on their own, so tours of the full exhibition typically last only 10 to 15 minutes. Requiring each student to write his

or her own tour script is a good accountability tool and can even be used as an assessment. However, some teachers prefer to work on this as a class and create one uniform tour script for the exhibition.

As students write, they should integrate the most important points from each exhibit into their tour script. Because they will be interacting with visitors during the tour, they should also consider how to meld Tilden's principles of interpretation into their script.

Practice Sessions

To practice for the opening, students can pair up and take turns giving each other a tour of the full exhibition. The student who plays the role of the museum visitor should ask questions that a visitor might ask. Before the opening event, students may provide tours for school groups. The field trip not only will be enjoyable for other students in your school and district, but it also will serve as a "dress rehearsal" for your students.

Randall Elementary School students practice their tour scripts and docent interaction techniques before opening night.

Assessing Knowledge

After students have had ample opportunity to learn the content of the entire exhibit, administer the project's summative assessments. Consider these examples:

- selected/constructed response test based on the statements of expected student learning for all exhibits
- extended written response test (post-test) with museum focus questions as prompts
- research write-up and graphic organizer for synthesizing research (completed during research)
- docent presentation for full museum (rubric for exhibit design, content portion; teacher-developed personal communication checklist for docent presentation)

Alternatively, you may prefer to administer assessments after the opening event.

Summary

Most students will work on one exhibit and have little knowledge about the other exhibits. In the days or week before the public opening, use the museum as a teaching tool to help students understand the full exhibition. Students can also teach one another the key points of their exhibit, illuminating the answer to their focus question.

In addition, developing and practicing docent activities and guiding peers on a complete tour of the exhibition can help students understand the content of the full museum. As the opening approaches, use summative assessments to determine the content knowledge that students have learned during the school museum project.

12

Opening the Museum to the Public

Second graders Nicholas, Andrew, Maria, and Abbey are in front of their exhibit, taking turns rehearsing their tour script. It is 6:15 p.m. and the school museum will soon be open to the public. The teacher asks students to review the opening night schedule and move to their first stations. Andrew walks to the front of the school museum where he will greet visitors and give them a copy of the student-created brochure explaining the museum's big idea and describing its exhibits. Nicholas walks to the "orientation" room where he will offer interested visitors a guided tour of the full exhibition. Maria and Abbey stay at their exhibit as docents. In 30 minutes, students will switch roles.

The students are all excited—and a little nervous. Tonight they are leaders. They will help peers, youngsters, and adults fully enjoy the school museum they worked so hard to create.

A public opening is a tangible end point for students' work and something concrete that justifies their effort. The responsibility of hosting such an event challenges students and encourages them to be accountable. As their teacher, you can offer support and perspective, but the challenge is part of the purpose of the school museum project.

The museum opening can also be a rewarding event for students. Peter, a student at Elmwood Elementary School, took pride in sharing his school's history museum with the public: "We actually got to learn our topic so well that we got to teach other people, and that was awesome. It was cool to know that we made a difference to the city of New Berlin and could teach them about our topic and . . . teach them not to repeat the mistakes [of] the past, but to learn from them. And that is what really made [me] probably one of the proudest students ever."

Student Roles

Students attend the opening as the proud exhibit designers, researchers, and curators of the completed museum. They also serve as museum staff and interact with visitors in a variety of ways. Students typically act as greeters, tour guides, docents and interpreters, presenters, and evaluators.

Greeters

Student greeters stationed at the entrance of the museum distribute programs or brochures and direct visitors to the exhibition. Brochures may include a summary of exhibition highlights, a map of the museum floor, a schedule of live events or demonstrations, and additional information about the museum topic.

Tour Guides

Students offer interested visitors a short guided tour of the museum, emphasizing key points from each exhibit. It's a good idea for each student to conduct at least one tour. Leading a tour will require students to learn about all the exhibits, not just their own. Tours should be short and to the point—most museum visitors want time to explore the exhibits independently.

Docents and Interpreters

Student docents or interpreters are stationed at each exhibit, encouraging visitor interaction by posing or answering questions. Students are knowledgeable about the material in their exhibit, but they may not know everything. When visitors ask questions that students cannot answer, it presents a new opportunity for learning. The history museum at Elmwood Elementary School included a mailbox at each exhibit. When students could not answer a question, they asked visitors

Randall Elementary School students interact with visitors on opening night.

to write their question and their e-mail address on a note card and put it in the mailbox. Visitors were promised a prompt e-mail response. Students answered the questions after the museum opening, which extended learning beyond the event.

Presenters

Some opening events offer live demonstrations or dramatizations staffed by students. The Fiesta del Arte Museum at Atwater Elementary School, for example, had an activity room where visitors created their own "make and take" art projects. Similarly, students at Atwater's Japanese Art and Culture Museum demonstrated printmaking, and Maple Avenue Elementary School students dramatized a Revolutionary War event by performing a short play based on a historical novel.

Based on the comments they received from visitors, student curators at Randall Elementary School were pleased with their final display.

Evaluators

Students can conduct simple visitor studies on opening night to assess the strengths and weaknesses of their completed exhibition. In this summative evaluation activity, student evaluators use observations, exit surveys, or questionnaires to determine what visitors liked about the exhibition and what they learned. Students later summarize this information and talk about what made certain exhibits highly appealing to visitors.

Observations. Students watch visitors as they tour the school museum. They keep track of visitor behavior, including the amount of time visitors spend at an exhibit, the amount of time visitors spend reading label copy at an exhibit, the exhibits (or text) where visitors talk to one another, and the path visitors take through the exhibition.

Exit surveys. As visitors leave the exhibition, students ask them a few simple questions, such as the following:

- What was the most enjoyable part of the visit for you?
- What was the most interesting part of our school museum?
- What did you learn about the museum topic?
- Do you think or feel differently about the topic as a result of visiting our school museum? How?
- What parts of this museum do you think we should take on a traveling exhibit?

Students write down visitors' responses for later review.

Questionnaires. Students ask visitors to complete a rating scale for selected exhibits. After the opening, students calculate the average rating for each exhibit and discuss the results. Figure 12.1 on p. 164 shows a sample questionnaire that your students may use for this purpose.

Plans for Opening Night

Entertainment events, family programs, demonstrations, and lectures often accompany the opening of professional museum exhibitions. School openings can also be fun and festive events, with special activities that complement the exhibition. Consider planning the opening early in the project to allow ample time to adequately prepare special activities.

Choosing Activities

Students will have many ideas for opening night activities. They can brainstorm a list of ideas and select activities to pursue. Criteria for selection may help narrow the list. For example, you may want to choose activities that enhance the educational value of the exhibition, that are fun for visitors, and that are feasible in terms of planning time and necessary resources. Activities for opening night might include the following:

Students at St. Paul's Elementary School were more invested in their school museum project knowing that visitors would attend an opening event.

• ribbon-cutting ceremony before museum opens (welcoming speech, introduction of key contributors, cutting of ribbon at museum entrance)
    • short play performed throughout the evening
    • strolling characters in period costume
    • musical performances throughout the evening
    • arts and crafts demonstration on the exhibit floor
    • hands-on workshops in a program room
    • ongoing activities, such as exhibit tours, orientations, and interpretation activities at each exhibit

Once opening night activities are selected, student planning committees can be established. There are several ways to organize planning committees:

Figure 12.1

Exhibit Questionnaire

Exhibit: _____

Trait	Excellent 5	Very Good 4	Adequate 3	Needs Improvement 2	Not Acceptable 1
Educational					
Informative					
Interesting					
Fun					
Easy to use					
Attractive					

Total score: _____

Schools advertise their museum openings in a variety of ways.

• Committees meet during class time. An exhibit team may form a committee if their exhibit includes a special activity. Committees may also be composed of students from various teams working together.

• Committees meet on their own time—after school or during lunch. Students do most of the work on their own under the direction of a teacher supervisor.

• Committees meet after school or during lunch as an enrichment club, run by a staff coordinator.

Teams may want to use a planning worksheet, such as the one shown in Figure 12.2, to keep track of activities and deadlines. You may want to model the planning process with students before small groups plan activities independently.

Figure 12.2
Activities Planning Worksheet

Step 1: List all tasks that need to be accomplished for your opening night activity.

Step 2: As a team, divide the tasks among yourselves.

Step 3: Create a time line for accomplishing the tasks and checking in with the team.

Step 4: Meet regularly to update your plan and make adjustments as needed.

Opening Night Activity: _____

Planning Committee Members: _____

Committee Task	Student	Due Date

Getting the Word Out

The opening night is an exciting culminating event for students. Advertise the event well in advance so that your students' hard work gets the audience it deserves. Send a press release to local and school newspapers and consider sending invitations to special guests—the school board, important community members, and friends of the school. Encourage as many people as possible to attend the opening to recognize the efforts of students. Examples of a press release and an invitation are shown in Figures 12.3 and 12.4 on pp. 166 and 167.

Creating a Schedule

An opening night schedule will keep students on track and aware of their responsibilities. Along with a master schedule, you may want to create individual schedules for all students so that they know what they are to do throughout the evening (see Figures 12.5 and 12.6 on pp. 168 and 169).

Figure 12.3
Press Release for Museum Opening

FOR IMMEDIATE RELEASE   FOR MORE INFORMATION CONTACT:
                                                          [contact person, phone number]

[name of exhibition], A STUDENT-DESIGNED MUSEUM, OPENS [date]

Through this innovative education project, students at **[name of school]** in **[name of city]** learned about **[museum topic]** in a uniquely "hands-on" fashion—by creating, designing, and building a museum about **[name of exhibition]**. A free public opening is scheduled as follows:

[name of exhibition]
[day, date, year]
[beginning and ending time]
[name of school]
[full address of school]

Visit on **[date and time]** to see these activities:

• [highlight of the museum]
• [highlight of the museum]
• [highlight of the museum]

Please plan to visit this exhibition on opening night or call to schedule a tour or interview prior to the opening.

After the Opening

If possible, keep the exhibition up beyond opening night for as long as you can. Many interested families and community members will appreciate the opportunity to visit the exhibition after the opening, especially if they were unable to attend that evening. Also, media coverage may inspire more visitors to come to your school.

Figure 12.4
Invitation to Museum Opening

You Are Invited
To the Opening of the

**American
Revolution
Museum**

Presented by the
5th Grade Class at
Maple Avenue Elementary School
Sussex, Wisconsin

The 5th Graders at
Maple Avenue Elementary
School
Invite You to Attend
A Special Opening Event

**American Revolution
Museum**

April 3, 2001
6:00–8:00 p.m.

Maple Avenue Elementary School
Sussex, Wisconsin

A seven-exhibit museum
designed and created by
5th grade students.

Please stop by for a
self-guided or student-led tour
of the exhibition.

Sadly, most exhibitions must eventually be dismantled. If you can, move portions of the school museum to another location so that you and other teachers can continue using the material as a teaching tool. Consider these ideas:

• Distribute components of your exhibit to various parts of your school (lobby, main office, grade level or department wing, and so on).

• Display your exhibit at another school in your district.

• Send your exhibit to a local museum or community center for display.

• Use portions of your exhibit in the continuing curriculum.

Figure 12.5

Opening Night Master Schedule

Greeters: Distribute program brochures as visitors arrive.

Time	Students (2)
6:00 p.m.	
6:15 p.m.	
6:30 p.m.	
6:45 p.m.	
7:00 p.m.	
7:15 p.m.	
7:30 p.m.	

Tour Guides: Provide guided tours of exhibition.

Time	Students
6:00 p.m.	
6:15 p.m.	
6:30 p.m.	
6:45 p.m.	
7:00 p.m.	
7:15 p.m.	
7:30 p.m.	

Docents and Interpreters: Interact with visitors at exhibits.

Exhibit	6:00	6:15	6:30	6:45	7:00	7:15	7:30
1							
2							
3							
4							
5							

Presenters: Perform during scheduled events.

Time	Team
6:00–6:30 p.m.	
6:30–7:00 p.m.	
7:00–7:30 p.m.	
7:30–8:00 p.m.	

Evaluators: Conduct visitor studies.

Exhibit	6:00	6:15	6:30	6:45	7:00	7:15	7:30
1							
2							
3							
4							
5							

Figure 12.6
Opening Night Individual Schedule

Name: Johnny Smith

Time	Responsibility
6:00–6:15 p.m.	Greeter
6:15–6:30 p.m.	Free—spend time with visiting family & friends
6:30–6:45 p.m.	Docent at Exhibit 2
6:45–7:00 p.m.	Docent at Exhibit 2
7:00–7:15 p.m.	Free—spend time with visiting family & friends
7:15–7:30 p.m.	Tour guide
7:30–7:45 p.m.	Evaluator
7:45–8:00 p.m.	Free—spend time with visiting family & friends

Students feel a tremendous sense of accomplishment in, and pride for, their museum. The days following the museum opening can be a letdown. A celebration provides an appropriate finish to this long-term and in-depth project.

One parent volunteered to sponsor an ice cream social after the opening of his daughter's school museum. The parent of a special needs student, he was delighted with the unique opportunity that the project provided for his daughter—she was a full participant in creating the school museum and worked collaboratively with her peers. All the students in her grade attended the event and had a wonderful time; the atmosphere was charged with energy, joy, and pride in a job well done. It was an important time for everyone to acknowledge and celebrate their accomplishments.

The celebration can be coordinated by a parent volunteer or it can be the job of a student committee (under the leadership of a teacher or other adult). You can invite parents and community members to this celebration, continuing the community spirit that the project engendered.

A simple program for the celebration might include the following:

• video or slide show presentation (pictures of students working throughout the process and visitors attending the opening night event)

• special recognition of all volunteers
• presentation of a student participation award
• student presentation of thank-you cards to important contributors (local museum staff, community volunteers, and the like)

As part of their celebration, Maple Avenue Elementary School 5th graders were photographed in front of their favorite school museum exhibit. The photos were then used on individual awards for student participants (see Figure 12.7). Award certificates are an effective way to acknowledge students and give them a tangible reminder of their success.

Figure 12.7
Student Participation Award

Congratulations to

[name of student]

for outstanding work on the
Maple Avenue Elementary School
Revolutionary War Museum

Summary

A public opening is a significant event for the school museum project. Students staff the museum as greeters, tour guides, docents, presenters, and evaluators—rotating roles during the event. Knowledge of this culminating responsibility motivates students' work throughout the project.

Student committees plan opening night activities, which may include short plays, strolling characters, demonstrations, musical performances, and workshops. The museum opening is an opportunity for the school and community to see the work of your students. Be sure to advertise the date and time of the opening early. Send a press release to the media and personal invitations to special guests. After the opening event, acknowledge the hard work and accomplishments of your students by hosting a celebration that includes parents, volunteers, and all who contributed to the school museum project.

Afterword

The school museum project is characterized by rigorous research, writing, and design; interdependent collaboration; and the representation of knowledge in visual, verbal, kinesthetic, tactile, dramatic, and written forms. Student curators work in a dynamic environment significantly different from that of the typical classroom. In this environment, students may see something new in themselves—their potential as independent and interdependent learners, leaders, creative thinkers, problem solvers, designers, builders, artists, and communicators.

I hope that the student-created museums described in this book have inspired you to start a project of your own. As you plan, don't feel as if you must do everything suggested; I don't know anyone who has. Start small and expand your scope; museum projects get easier after you have done one for the first time. Even a small, well-planned project is sure to encourage your students' creativity and reveal their competence and potential to their peers, to their parents, to their community, and to themselves.

Good luck!

Appendixes

Appendix A
Agendas for Planning Meetings

The following sample agendas may assist teams in planning for the school museum project. Details on the planning activities included in the agendas can be found in Chapter 3, unless otherwise specified. An overview of the curriculum planning process is shown in Figure 3.1 on p. 24.

Meeting 1: Select a Museum Topic

- Review the different approaches for selecting a museum topic.
- Brainstorm ideas for consideration and list them on poster paper.
- Discuss each idea, allowing team members to advocate for their ideas.
- Select your topic.

Before Meeting 2

- Review the academic content standards related to your museum topic, making note of the most relevant standards.
- Locate and read relevant professional materials to expand your knowledge of the museum topic.
- Locate and review ways in which professional local or national museums have approached your topic.

Meeting 2: Share Information and Develop a Big Idea

- Share impressions of the standards review, selecting the academic content standards that your museum project will address.

- Share information from the review of professional materials.
- Share information from the review of professional local or national exhibitions.
- Write a "big idea" for your exhibition.

Before Meeting 3

- Conduct the "What do you know?" and "What do you wonder?" activity with students, compiling results to share with the team.

Meeting 3: Create an Affinity Diagram

- Share results from the "know and wonder" activity; note student misconceptions, which you may want to address in focus questions, statements of expected student learning, or student research questions.
- Create an affinity diagram with the springboard question "What will students learn as a result of being involved in this museum project?" (See Figure 3.3 on p. 34 for an example of a completed affinity diagram.)
- Decide whether you will engage parent groups in affinity diagramming. If so, determine the time and place for sessions.

Before Meeting 4

- Conduct parent affinity diagramming sessions and type up the results.
- Arrange for a full-day planning session, if possible, to cover the material in Meetings 4–10.

Meeting 4: Develop a Story Line and Focus Questions

- Review the affinity diagrams and know and wonder charts (including student misconceptions).
- Discuss the "story worth telling"—what, of all that is possible, are the important messages the museum should communicate? Do not talk about exhibit ideas at this point; focus on the key ideas for inclusion in the school museum.
- Write a story line for your exhibition.
- Translate story line statements into focus questions.

Meeting 5: Write Statements of Expected Student Learning

- Write each focus question at the top of a sheet of paper or poster paper.

• List brainstorming results, student misconceptions, selected standards, and new teacher knowledge under the appropriate focus question. Some of your early work will not fit under a specific focus question, and you may decide not to include it.

• Use the ideas under each focus question to write statements of expected student learning.

Meeting 6: Write Student Research Questions

• Review the statements of expected student learning from prior meeting.

• Create a set of student research questions for the statements of expected student learning.

Meeting 7: Review Standards Alignment

• Review the student research questions aligned to the statements of expected student learning and focus questions.

• Review the state and local academic content standards related to the school museum topic and select those that match the statements of expected student learning and student research questions.

• Make adjustments in the statements of expected student learning and student research questions if necessary for better standards alignment.

Meeting 8: Consider Assessments

• Review the learning targets for school museum projects and make adjustments if necessary (see Chapter 4).

• Review the matrix shown in Figure 4.2 on pp. 48–49 and decide which assessment methods you will use to evaluate student achievement of the learning targets.

• Develop a grading plan (see Figure 4.3 on p. 50).

• Review strategies for ongoing, student-involved assessment and decide which ones you will use to provide opportunities for students to monitor their work in progress (see Chapter 4).

Meeting 9: Plan for Museum Visit and Invite Parent Involvement

• Discuss possible field trip locations and contact a museum educator or curator to arrange a behind-the-scenes program (see Chapter 6).

• Brainstorm possible parent involvement opportunities (see Chapter 2) and write a letter to parents about your project (see Figure 2.1 on p. 17).

Meeting 10: Schedule Instructional Activities

• Determine regular collaborative meeting times so teachers can plan, solve problems, and reflect on students' work in the school museum project.

• Select a date for the opening of your school museum and set a general schedule for instructional activities. (See Figure 5.1 on pp. 64–65 for an overview of the instructional process.)

Appendix B
Student-Involved Assessment Strategies

Introduce the Museum Project

Envisioning High-Quality Work

- Rewrite the museum project learning targets in language your students will understand.
- Help students brainstorm features of high-quality work for each target.
- Create a teamwork rubric with your students (see Figure 5.5 on p. 78).
- Discuss what students already know about good and bad teamwork to further their understanding of each quality listed on the rubric.

Achieving High-Quality Work

- Administer a pre-test (an extended written response test or a selected/constructed response test) on museum focus questions.
- Throughout the project, design lessons to focus on one aspect of quality at a time. (See the mini-lesson on teamwork in Chapter 5 for an example.)

Visit a Professional Museum

Envisioning High-Quality Work

- Create an exhibit design rubric with your students based on an examination of the traits of effective professional exhibits (see Figure 8.1 on pp. 116–117).

• Show or discuss models of strong and weak exhibits and use the rubric to assess them.

Achieving High-Quality Work

• Ask students to evaluate their teamwork skills based on their small-group experience at the professional museum.

• Encourage students to share specific examples of good teamwork behavior and to link them to rubric traits.

Research the Museum Topic

Envisioning High-Quality Work

• Discuss what students already know about good and bad research skills to further their understanding of each quality listed on the research rubric (see Figure 7.1 on pp. 92–93).

• Show models of strong and weak research notes and use the rubric to assess them.

• Model the research process, being sure to show the predictable challenges.

Achieving High-Quality Work

• Use guided practice and focused mini-lessons to teach research skills.

• Ask students to assess their research work using the research rubric.

• Help students identify their strengths and goals using the three-minute conference strategy (see Figure 4.4 on p. 56).

• Offer students descriptive feedback using the traits of the research rubric.

• Encourage reflective student writing to address what students have learned and what questions they still have.

• Ask students to summarize their learning and set goals for future learning. Consider using the prompt "I have learned . . . I need to work on . . . "

• Have students keep a portfolio of assessment activities to reflect on their growth. Consider asking them to respond to the reflective writing prompt "I have become a better researcher this year. I used to . . . , but now I . . ."

• Ask students to create several selected/constructed response test items highlighting key points related to their exhibit focus questions.

• Require students to give short presentations to their classmates highlighting the most important points found in their research.

Design the Exhibits

Envisioning High-Quality Work

• Show models of strong and weak professional exhibits and use the exhibit design rubric to assess them (see Figure 8.1 on p. 116–117).

Achieving High-Quality Work

• Teach mini-lessons on various traits from the exhibit design rubric.

• Ask exhibit teams to assess their work using the rubric.

• Help students identify their strengths and goals using the three-minute conference strategy (see Figure 4.4 on p. 56).

• Offer students descriptive feedback using the traits of the exhibit design rubric.

• Model the revision process by showing students how you would revise an exhibit and letting them revise similar but different material.

• Ask students to analyze samples of your work and make suggestions for improvement. Revise your work using their advice and have them review it again.

• Ask students to revise their own exhibit design based on their self-assessment.

Write for a Museum Audience

Envisioning High-Quality Work

• Discuss what students already know about good and bad label copy to further their understanding of each quality listed on the label copy rubric (see Figure 9.1 on pp. 138–139).

• Show models of strong and weak label copy and use the rubric to assess them.

• Model the process of writing from research notes, being sure to show the predictable challenges.

Achieving High-Quality Work

- Teach mini-lessons on various traits from the label copy rubric.
- Ask students to assess their label copy using the rubric.
- Help students identify their strengths and goals using the three-minute conference strategy (see Figure 4.4 on p. 56).
- Offer descriptive feedback using the traits of the label copy rubric.
- Model the revision process by showing students how you would revise label copy and letting them revise similar but different material.
- Ask students to analyze samples of your work and make suggestions for improvement. Revise your work using their advice and have them review it again.
- Ask students to revise their own label copy based on their self-assessment.
- Ask students to summarize their learning and set goals for future learning. Consider using the prompt "I have learned . . . I need to work on . . . "

Construct the Exhibition

Envisioning High-Quality Work

- Discuss what students already know about good and bad planning and teamwork to further their understanding of each quality listed on the teamwork rubric (see Figure 5.5 on p. 78).
- Describe examples of strong and weak organization, planning, and teamwork skills and help students brainstorm strategies for keeping the museum project on track.
- Model the process of planning, being sure to show the predictable challenges.

Achieving High-Quality Work

- Ask students to assess their teamwork skills using the teamwork rubric.
- Help students identify their strengths and goals using the three-minute conference strategy (see Figure 4.4 on p. 56).
- Ask students to summarize their learning and set goals for future learning. Consider using the prompt "I have learned . . . I need to work on . . . "

Learn the Full Exhibition

Envisioning High-Quality Work

• Help students brainstorm characteristics of high-quality docents and interpreters.

• Create a rubric for interpretation with your students.

• Model the process of interpreting exhibits, being sure to show the predictable challenges.

Achieving High-Quality Work

• Ask students to assess their skill as docents (using the interpretation rubric, if you have developed one).

• Offer descriptive feedback as students practice docent skills.

• Help students identify their strengths and goals using the three-minute conference strategy (see Figure 4.4 on p. 56).

• Ask students to compare their pre-test and post-test responses and to explain what they have learned.

• Have students assess their personal communication skills as greeters, tour guides, docents and interpreters, presenters, and evaluators.

References

Arter, J., & Chappuis, J. (Presenters). (2001). *Student-involved performance assessment* [Videotape]. Portland, OR: Assessment Training Institute.

Arter, J., & McTighe, J. (2001). *Scoring rubrics in the classroom: Using performance criteria for assessing and improving student performance.* Thousand Oaks, CA: Corwin Press.

Barell, J. (2003). *Developing more curious minds.* Alexandria, VA: Association for Supervision and Curriculum Development.

Black, P., & Wiliam, D. (1998). Inside the black box: Raising standards through classroom assessment. *Phi Delta Kappan, 80*(2), 139–144, 146–148.

Bunting, E. (1991). *Fly away home.* New York: Clarion Books.

Covington, M. V. (1992). *Making the grade: A self-worth perspective on motivation and school reform.* New York: Cambridge University Press.

Dierking, L., & Pollock, W. (1998, July/August). Front-end studies: Where the museum and the community meet. *ASTC Dimensions.* Available at http://www.astc.org/pubs/dimensions/1998/jul-aug/frontend.htm

Falk, J., & Dierking, L. (1992). *The museum experience.* Washington, DC: Whalesback Books.

Gardner, H. (1983). *Frames of mind: The theory of multiple intelligences.* New York: Basic Books.

Gardner, H. (1993). *Multiple intelligences: The theory in practice.* New York: Basic Books.

Gilman, C. (2003). *Lewis and Clark: Across the divide.* Washington, DC: Smithsonian Books; and St. Louis, MO: Missouri Historical Society.

Hamilton School District. (1997). *Hamilton School District writing program.* Waukesha County, WI: Author.

Hamilton School District. (2000). *Hamilton School District social studies curriculum, grade 5: United States history, pre-Columbus to the Civil War.* Waukesha County, WI: Author.

Harmin, M. (1994). *Inspiring active learning.* Alexandria, VA: Association for Supervision and Curriculum Development.

Henderson, A., & Kaeppler, A. L. (1997). *Exhibiting dilemmas: Issues of representation at the Smithsonian.* Washington, DC: Smithsonian Institution Press.

Marzano, R. J., Norford, J. S., Paynter, D. E., Pickering, D. J., & Gaddy, B. B. (2001). *A handbook for classroom instruction that works.* Alexandria, VA: Association for Supervision and Curriculum Development.

Marzano, R. J., Pickering, D. J., & Pollock, J. E. (2001). *Classroom instruction that works: Research-based strategies for increasing student achievement.* Alexandria, VA: Association for Supervision and Curriculum Development.

McGovern, A. (1999). *If you lived 100 years ago.* New York: Scholastic.

Michalko, M. (1991). *Thinkertoys: A handbook of business creativity for the '90s.* Berkeley, CA: Ten Speed Press.

National Council for the Social Studies. (1994). *The curriculum standards for social studies: Expectations of excellence.* Silver Spring, MD: Author.

Partnership for 21st Century Skills. (2004). *The road to 21st century learning: A policymakers' guide to 21st century skills.* Washington, DC: Author. Available from http://www.21stcenturyskills.org

Pratt, K. J. (1992). *A walk in the rainforest.* Nevada City, CA: Dawn Publications.

Pratt, K. J. (1994). *A swim through the sea.* Nevada City, CA: Dawn Publications.

Rogovin, P. (2001). *The research workshop: Bringing the world into your classroom.* Portsmouth, NH: Heinemann.

Schauble, L., Leinhardt, G., & Martin, L. (1997). A framework for organizing a cumulative research agenda in informal learning contexts. *Journal of Museum Education, 22*(2&3), 3–8.

Senge, P., Ross, R., Smith, B., Roberts, C., & Kleiner, A. (1994). *The fifth discipline fieldbook: Strategies and tools for building a learning organization.* New York: Doubleday.

Serrell, B. (1996). *Exhibit labels: An interpretative approach.* Walnut Creek, CA: AltaMira Press.

Starnes, B. A., & Carone, A. (with Paris, C.). (2002). (Rev. ed.). *From thinking to doing: The Foxfire core practices.* Mountain City, GA: Foxfire Fund.

Stiggins, R. (2001). *Student-involved classroom assessment.* (3rd ed.). Upper Saddle River, NJ: Merrill Education/Prentice Hall.

Stiggins, R., Arter, J., Chappuis, J., & Chappuis, S. (2004). *Classroom assessment for student learning: Doing it right—using it well.* Portland, OR: Assessment Training Institute.

Tilden, F. (1977). *Interpreting our heritage.* (3rd ed.). Chapel Hill: University of North Carolina Press.

Torp, L., & Sage, S. (1998). *Problems as possibilities.* Alexandria, VA: Association for Supervision and Curriculum Development.

Wiggins, G. (1993). *Assessing student performance: Exploring the purpose and limits of testing.* San Francisco: Jossey-Bass.

Wiggins, G. (1998). *Educative assessment: Designing assessments to inform and improve student performance.* San Francisco: Jossey-Bass.

Wiggins, G., & McTighe, J. (1998). *Understanding by Design.* Alexandria, VA: Association for Supervision and Curriculum Development.

Wisconsin Department of Public Instruction. (1998). *Wisconsin's model academic standards.* Madison, WI: Author.

Index

Page numbers followed by *f* indicate illustrations.

About the Author

Linda D'Acquisto has more than 20 years of experience in education as a former classroom teacher, curriculum coordinator, director of instruction, and museum educator. Now a full-time consultant, Linda offers professional development workshops for teachers interested in learning more about the school museum process. She also works with  school districts and other educational organizations in the areas of program evaluation, classroom assessment, professional learning community development, school improvement planning, professional development planning, and leadership training. She has a bachelor's degree in behavioral disabilities and a master's degree in curriculum and instruction, both from the University of Wisconsin–Madison.

Linda can be reached at ldacquisto@msn.com or through her Web site at www.kidcurators.com.

Related ASCD Resources

At the time of publication, the following ASCD resources were available; for the most up-to-date information about ASCD resources, go to www.ascd.org. ASCD stock numbers are noted in parentheses.

Audio

Empowering Students to Influence Their World by Laurie Nunnelee, Diane Puckett, and James Wilkowski (Audiotape #204193; CD #504327)

Igniting the Enthusiasm for Learning Through Project-Based Instruction by Mark Aguirre and Tom Atwell (Audiotape #203148; CD #503241)

Implementing Standards into a Project-Based Learning Curriculum: What Does It Take? by Mark Aguirre and Tom Atwell (Audiotape #202164)

Problem-Based Learning by William J. Stepien (2 Audiotapes #203093)

Multimedia

Problem-Based Learning Across the Curriculum: An ASCD Professional Inquiry Kit by William J. Stepien and Shelagh Gallagher (8 Activity Folders and 1 Videotape #997148)

Networks

Visit the ASCD Web site (www.ascd.org) and click on About ASCD. Go to the section on Networks for information about professional educators who have formed groups around topics such as "Multiple Intelligences" and "Problem-Based Learning." Look in the Network Directory for current facilitators' addresses and phone numbers.

Online Courses

Visit the ASCD Web site (www.ascd.org) for the following professional development opportunities:
Understanding by Design: An Introduction by John Brown (#PD03OC29)

Print Products

Developing More Curious Minds by John Barell (#101246)

Educational Leadership, September 2002: Do Students Care About Learning? (Entire Issue #102305)

Educational Leadership, September 2004: Teaching for Meaning (Entire Issue #105028)

Increasing Student Learning Through Multimedia Projects by Michael Simkins, Karen Cole, Fern Tavalin, and Barbara Means (#102112)

Making the Most of Understanding by Design by John L. Brown (#103110)

Problems as Possibilities: Problem-Based Learning for K–16 Education, 2nd Edition by Linda Torp and Sara Sage (#101064)

Understanding by Design, Expanded 2nd Edition by Grant Wiggins and Jay McTighe (#103055)

Understanding by Design Professional Development Workbook by Jay McTighe and Grant Wiggins (#103056)

Video

The Lesson Collection, Tape 14: *Environmental Project—Internet (Middle School)* (Videotape #400066)

Problem-Based Learning Video Series: *Using Problems to Learn* and *Designing Problems for Learning* (2 Videotapes and Facilitator's Guide written by William J. Stepien #497172)

For more information, visit us on the World Wide Web (www.ascd.org), send an e-mail message to member@ascd.org, call the ASCD Service Center (1-800-933-ASCD or 703-578-9600, then press 2), send a fax to 703-575-5400, or write to Information Services, ASCD, 1703 N. Beauregard St., Alexandria, VA 22311-1714 USA.

2712
Gift